Kingdom Dynamics

Volume 2

Growing in Sonship

By

Dr. Ron M. Horner

Kingdom Dynamics
Volume 2

Growing in Sonship

By
Dr. Ron M. Horner

LifeSpring International Ministries
PO Box 5847
Pinehurst, North Carolina 28374
RonHorner.com

Kingdom Dynamics – Volume 2

Growing in Sonship

Copyright © 2023 Dr. Ron M. Horner

Scripture is taken from the New King James Version®. Copyright © 1982 by Thomas Nelson. Used by permission. All rights reserved. (Unless otherwise noted.)

Scripture quotations marked (TPT) are from The Passion Translation®, Copyright © 2017, 2018 by BroadStreet Publishing Group, LLC. Used by permission. All rights reserved. ThePassionTranslation.com

Scripture marked (THE MIRROR) is taken from The Mirror Study Bible by Francois du Toit. Copyright © 2021 All Rights Reserved. Used by permission of The Author.

All rights reserved. This book is protected by the copyright laws of the United States of America. This book may not be copied or reprinted for commercial gain or profit. The use of short quotations or occasional page copying for personal, or group study is permitted and encouraged. Permission will be granted upon request.

Any trademarks mentioned or used are the property of their respective owners.

Requests for bulk sales discounts, editorial permissions, or other information should be addressed to:

LifeSpring Publishing
PO Box 5847
Pinehurst, NC 28374 USA

Additional copies available at
www.LifeSpringPublishing.com

ISBN 13 TP: 978-1-953684-36-3
ISBN 13 eBook: 978-1-953684-41-7

Cover Design by Darian Horner Design
(www.darianhorner.com)
Image: 123rf.com #137529428

First Edition: May 2023

10 9 8 7 6 5 4 3 2 1

Printed in the United States of America

Table of Contents

Acknowledgements i

Characters in this Book iii

Preface v

Chapter 1 The Kingdom Dynamic
of New Knowledge 1

Chapter 2 The Kingdom Dynamic
of Joy 3

Chapter 3 The Kingdom Dynamic
of Engaging Your Spirit 7

Chapter 4 The Kingdom Dynamic
of the Weapon of Patience 19

Chapter 5 The Kingdom Dynamic
of Being Uncompromised 25

Chapter 6 The Kingdom Dynamic
of Possessing Your Mountaintop 29

Chapter 7 The Kingdom Dynamic
of Trusting Your Spirit 35

Chapter 8 The Kingdom Dynamic
of Walking on Water 39

Chapter 9 The Kingdom Dynamic
of Strength & Adjudication 43

Chapter 10 The Kingdom Dynamic
of a Molecular Walk...................................... 47

Chapter 11 The Kingdom Dynamic
of Your Lease Agreement 51

Chapter 12 The Kingdom Dynamic
of Considering the Stars 55

Chapter 13 The Kingdom Dynamic
of Sacred Ground 59

Chapter 14 The Kingdom Dynamic
of Dimensional Work.................................... 63

Chapter 15 The Kingdom Dynamic
of Exchange 67

Chapter 16 The Kingdom Dynamic
of the Peace Bond... 81

Chapter 17 The Kingdom Dynamic
of the Spirit of Understanding..................... 85

Chapter 18 The Kingdom Dynamic
of the Entity of Prudence............................. 97

Chapter 19 The Kingdom Dynamic
of Grace Abounding................................... 103

Chapter 20 The Kingdom Dynamic
of Digging Deeper...................................... 109

Chapter 21 The Kingdom Dynamic
of Illumination 115

Chapter 22 The Kingdom Dynamic
of Thirst 121

Chapter 23 The Kingdom Dynamic
of Wisdom Constructs.. 125

Chapter 24 The Kingdom Dynamic
of Molecular Widgets.. 133

Chapter 25 The Kingdom Dynamic
of Freedom from Fragility... 143

Chapter 26 The Kingdom Dynamic
of the Expanse of the Kingdom 147

Chapter 27 The Kingdom Dynamic
of Serendipity.. 155

Chapter 28 The Kingdom Dynamic
of Ruling as a Son... 161

Chapter 29 The Kingdom Dynamic
of a Quieted & Enlarged Soul 165

Chapter 30 The Kingdom Dynamic
of Letting the Glory Stand Up.................................... 169

Chapter 31 The Kingdom Dynamic
of the Spirit of Excellence.. 181

Chapter 32 The Kingdom Dynamic
of Stepping into Position.. 191

Chapter 33 The Kingdom Dynamic
of Projected Glory 201

Chapter 34 The Kingdom Dynamic
of a Turning Tide.. 211

Chapter 35 The Kingdom Dynamic
of the Wellspring of Life.. 217

Chapter 36 The Kingdom Dynamic
of the Need to Govern Voices 223

Chapter 37 The Kingdom Dynamic
of Timing Devices... 229

Chapter 38 The Kingdom Dynamic
of Freedom from Taxation & Slavery 243

Chapter 39 The Kingdom Dynamic
of the Redemption Center... 253

Chapter 40 The Kingdom Dynamic
of Recognizing Your Gift... 263

Chapter 41 The Kingdom Dynamic
of Being in the Father's Hands 267

Chapter 42 The Kingdom Dynamic
of Going Deeper 271

Chapter 43 The Kingdom Dynamic
of the Lens of Promise 279

Chapter 44 The Kingdom Dynamic
of Being One with Creation 283

Chapter 45 The Kingdom Dynamic
of Good Fruit 289

Chapter 46 The Kingdom Dynamic
of Knowing the Gates of Hell Won't Prevail............. 291

Chapter 47 The Kingdom Dynamic
of a Governing Mantle 295

Chapter 48 The Kingdom Dynamic
of the Master's Key... 299

Chapter 49 The Kingdom Dynamic
of Quantum—the Purest Form of Intimacy............... 311

Chapter 50 The Kingdom Dynamic
of Ordered Steps.. 319

Appendix A.. 325

The Kingdom Dynamic
of Accessing the Realms of Heaven.......................... 325

References 331

Description 333

About the Author 335

Other Books by Dr. Ron M. Horner............................... 337

Acknowledgements

Our Heavenly Father has again been wonderfully gracious to surround me with an exceptional team who are committed to seeing the Kingdom expand upon the earth through this ministry. May they step into revelation in new measure. May they have intimate knowledge of the goodness of the Father, and may they arise to the full stature of the measure of Christ in them. Be world changers team, be world changers!

———·———

Characters in this Book

In this book, we introduce you to several entities who assisted us in its writing:

Adina – Ron Horner's wife.

Albert – Angel who assists Sandhills Ecclesia.

Alicia – A woman in white who serves as our Personnel Advisor.

Bartholomew – A Man in White who assisted us.

Ezekiel – The Chief Angel over LifeSpring.

Enoch – A man in white mentioned in Genesis and Jude

David – David Porter III is Lead Apostle of Sandhills Ecclesia and an accountant on our team.

Gail – A woman in white who assists Sandhills Ecclesia.

George – A man in white who assists in the financial affairs of LifeSpring.

Joseph – A man in white.

Jonathan – Angel assisting Sandhills Ecclesia.

Knowledge – (Spirit of Knowledge) one of the seven spirits of God.

Lydia – A woman in white who assists LifeSpring.

Malcolm – A man in white who is the Headmaster of CourtsNet.

Moses – The patriarch who is also a man in white.

Seth – A man in white who assists the Sandhills Ecclesia intercessors.

Stephanie – My current Executive Assistant.

Understanding (Spirit of Understanding) – One of the seven spirits of God.

Wisdom (Spirit of Wisdom) – One of the seven spirits of God.

———·———

Preface

King David met us as we engaged Heaven, and when asked what he had for us that day, he replied, "Spectacles."

Stephanie replied, "Well, David, that has two meanings to me: spectacles you see out of and something being made a spectacle of. Which one are we talking about?"

King David asked her, "Didn't you just receive some new glasses? Some new lenses?" (The Help Desk had given us new lenses the day before).

Stephanie replied, "I did."

King David remarked, "Well, why don't we look through those lenses today."

Stephanie exclaimed, "I say yes, King David!

Angels, I commission you to help me see through these lenses. Thank you, Father, for the new lenses that allow us to see more clearly.

King David explained, "Son, I'm going to take you on a journey."

Stephanie remarked, "I thought all of these were journeys. He is laughing. I see the picture of a woman on the back of a donkey or a horse and a man beside her. Now, my immediate thought was Mary and Joseph while she was pregnant with Jesus. Am I correct in this summation?"

King David asked what lens Mary was looking through on that journey. It was the lens of the promise of what the angel had said to her.

He then asked what lens Joseph was looking through on the same journey. Was he looking through the same lens as Mary? They both had a promise from the angel. What lens would you say most would look through on this journey? Most of the sons hear the promise but don't view it through the lens of the promise on their journey. Why is that?

It could be because of false indoctrination, false teachings in the church, or could it be that we take these Scriptures for granted? We've heard them and we've heard about the promise, but we don't walk in it or even believe it is for us.

It is around sonship. In the natural, if a father makes a promise to his son, there is an expectancy of the fulfillment of that promise from the father to the son. In most instances, wouldn't the son know to expect the promise? Why do we, as sons, not honestly believe the promise through the lens of our Heavenly Father?

We must take our rightful positions as sons.

Sons must look through the lens of the Father, through the promise of the Father, hold onto it, know it, experience it, taking our rightful place as sons because every good and perfect gift is from the Father.

Stephanie prayed,

Father, I would like to say thank you for the lenses. Please help us, as sons, see the promises through the lens you have given us. Help us experience the promise through the lens you have given us. Please help us take our rightful place as sons, knowing and expecting the promise.

When we realize that we are sons of God, we will experience life in a new dimension. Whereas events often move us, we no longer accept everything that is happening as the will of God for us. We will begin to walk in who we are and whose we are. As sons, we will learn to govern our realms, territories, dimensions, and stars.

Realizing that we don't have to live with a victim's mindset is refreshing. Instead, we know—we are fully convinced that we are those who can exercise authority on the earth and in the heavens.

A few years ago, something within me shifted after participating in a series of meetings in Western North Carolina. Whereas I had been living defensively, that was no more. I stopped praying defensive prayers. I stopped going through the charismatic calisthenics many go through to stay in victory. I knew I could govern things in my life and the realms around me. No longer was I trying to keep the devil at bay.

Before this, I had been concerned about what he was up to—what trick he had to release on me next; now, he had reason to be concerned about me. I no longer had to see what he was doing to know how to respond. No, he was responding to me.

Friends, that is incredibly liberating. It was not born of my soul; rather, it finally registered in my spirit. I learned what John wrote in 1 John 3:2:

Beloved, now are we the sons of God....

Such a difference it makes.

In this book, you will read of engagements with Heaven I experienced with members of the LifeSpring Team. All of us were blessed by these engagements. They will help you in your grasp of the sonship that is your possession.

In some of the epistles of Paul, we find him opening those letters by addressing the saints and the faithful.

*Saints are those who have
stepped into their sonship
and are learning to govern.*

The faithful have just stepped into their journey with the Father, but the concept of sonship has not yet registered within them. If you have not transitioned from the faithful to the saints, may it occur as you read this book.

Take your rightful place as sons!

Chapter 1
The Kingdom Dynamic of New Knowledge

As we engaged Heaven, we heard the verse, "the joy of the Lord is your strength" (Nehemiah 8:10).

Then Enoch, a man in white who had joined us, asked, "What's the verse right after that?"

> *So the Levites calmed all the people, saying, 'Be quiet, for this day is holy; do not be grieved.' (Nehemiah 8:11)*

He asked, "Why would anyone want to partake of sorrow when we have Heaven every day?"

Heavenly encounters bring the joy of the Lord.

"It is our strength. Strengthen ourselves daily. If we had dung or pie sitting before us daily, which would we partake of?

Why would we not partake of Heaven every day? It's where you will draw strength. It *is* the pie in the sky, but it is not where you will find just riches.

To many, 'Pie in the sky' means unattainable, but this *is attainable*. If the joy of the Lord is our strength and Heaven is where we find it, what will we find beyond that?

Father is putting proper processes in place. He is putting things and people in place. As this revelation comes to light, as we seek first the Kingdom of God, all these things will be added to us. People may have this information, but they must utilize it. It's for our growth.

---
*Heaven has expectations of the sons.
With new growth, there can be
new knowledge.*

Some sons are catching up, but they need to know that there's an expectation because, with much knowledge, much is required.

Chapter 2
The Kingdom Dynamic of Joy

In this engagement with Heaven, Stephanie and I found ourselves riding in a small sports car. We stopped, and Malcolm appeared and asked, "Did you like that?"

Stephanie asked, "What were we doing in a sports car?"

He said, "It's fun. It brings excitement. It takes you to new places, and it's fast. (I was driving, by the way).

Stephanie remarked, "And I wasn't scared at all, but we *were* going fast."

Malcolm was in the back of the car with us, a convertible, and we found ourselves driving through a glorious landscape with lots of wheat fields. We saw a lot of harvesting on one side of the road, but on the other were pastures, horses, and water.

"Where are you taking us, Malcolm?" Stephanie asked.

He said, "You know about a joy ride, right?"

"Yes," she replied.

Malcolm continued, "Well, let's concentrate on the joy of the moment. The joy in the moment where there is no drudgery, complications, or dread. This is Kingdom Dynamics—the ability to be with the Father in Heaven, in joy and enjoying."

We then stopped and got out of the car.

There is so much the Father wants to give to his children. The gleaning and the leaning are an integral part of it all.

The joy is what he wants us to revel in—to stand in.

The simplicity of being able to step in is still very profound—stepping over or through the veil into a place where there is joy unspeakable, unrelenting joy.

Today's instruction was simply a reminder.

Keep it fun to ensure we are having fun. Heaven is saying to make sure we find the joy—keep it in front of us, walk in it, as we step over into this realm and walk in the joy ever before us.

Are we finding joy in what we are doing? If not, we are stepping in with the wrong pretenses—we are soul-forward instead of *spirit-forward*. There is only joy in the realms of Heaven. It is a place of answers and truths. Souls will get caught up in the works of the courts.

The freshness of stepping in very childlike is vital.

Even in Heaven, there is joy in the smallest things.

As we step into Heaven, everything in Heaven that has breath praises the Lord. It is not an instruction about praising the Lord. When we step in, we know that that is what we want to do, but it is an instruction about coming in childlike joy, expecting joy, expecting truth, expecting answers, not anything of works. Freedom is in Heaven. Delight in the Kingdom of Heaven. Delight in the Kingdom Dynamics.

We are growing, and there will be times when Heaven will remind us of these things. We have had a reminder of joy. We have had a reminder of truth.

Father, we thank You for the joy of Heaven. We thank You for the simplicity of stepping over in the now through the profound nature of what Jesus did for us that has allowed us to be in Your presence in Heaven. We find great joy in that Father. We find great joy in being able to come in as a child, knowing that You, Father, with truth— all truth will give us the answers that we need, the peace that we seek, and ultimately the joy that You bring in working on behalf of Your Kingdom

Father. Thank You for all of those that work on behalf of LifeSpring. Thank You for the reminder.

———·———

Chapter 3
The Kingdom Dynamic
of Engaging Your Spirit

A significant pathway to living out our sonship is *our cooperation with Heaven and the domination of our spirit*. As a ministry, we teach how to live spirit-forward—to have our spirit be the dominant part of us. Heaven wants us to learn to live from our spirit instead of living dominated by our soul or body. To do so, we must change our vantage point.

In Colossians 3, Paul writes:

[1] See yourselves co-raised with Christ. Now ponder with persuasion the consequence of your co-inclusion in him. Relocate yourselves mentally. Engage your thoughts with throne room realities where you are co-seated with Christ in the executive authority of God's right hand. [2] Becoming affectionately acquainted with throne

room thoughts will keep you from being distracted again by the earthly [soul-ruled] realm.

("Set your minds upon the things that are above and not upon the things below." (MIRROR)

(RSV. Whatever you face in your daily lives, acquaint yourselves with the greater reality—the things that are above.)

Heaven is the real; earth is the vapor!

We have wasted so much time trying to get there (to Heaven), when "there" is where we are to begin with. Do not engage the energy of the things that are below.

Don't use bandwidth

for the unnecessary

In the article "Building a Defense Against Lies,"[1] Heaven talked about maximizing our bandwidth.

Always reserve the majority

of our bandwidth for our spirit

to operate from.

We are not keeping any score of what seems so obvious to the senses on the surface; it is fleeting

---

[1] Look for the article on www.courtsofheavenwebinars.com.

and irrelevant; it is the unseen eternal realm within us which has our full attention and captivates our gaze. (2 Corinthians 4:18)

A renewed mind conquers
the space previously occupied
by worthless pursuits and habits.

Continuing with Colossians 3:3:

Your union with his death broke the association with that world; see yourselves located in a fortress where your life is hidden with Christ in God (or the secret of your life is your union with Christ in God). (MIRROR)

[Occupy your mind with this new order of life; you died when Jesus died; whatever defined you before defines you no more. Christ, in whom the fullness of deity dwells, defines you now. Change your position of thought.]

[Risen, then, with Christ you must lift your thoughts above where Christ now sits at the right hand of God, you must be heavenly minded; not earthly minded, you have undergone death, and your life is hidden away now with Christ in God. Christ is your life, when He is made manifest you are made manifest in His glory. (Knox Translation)]

⁴ The unveiling of Christ, as defining our lives, immediately implies that, what is evident in him, is equally mirrored in you. The exact life on exhibit in Christ is now repeated in us. We are included in the same bliss and joined-oneness with him; just as his life reveals you, your life reveals him. (MIRROR)

Every time Christ is revealed,
we are being co-revealed in his glory.
We are co-revealed in the same bliss.

In him we live and move and have our being; In us He lives and moves and has His being. (Acts 17:28)

⁵ Consider the members of your body as dead and buried towards everything related to the porn industry, sensual uncleanness, longing for forbidden things, lust and greed, which are just another form of idol worship. (Idol worship is worshipping a distorted image of yourself.)

⁶ These distorted expressions are in total contradiction to God's design and desire for your life.

Change Your Clothes

Galatians 3 reads,

26 What Jesus Christ believes to be true about you is the final confirmation of mankind's redeemed sonship. His faith is the only valid reference to your belief. 27 To be immersed in Christ is to be fully clothed with him. He is your brand-new wardrobe confirming your sonship.

[(From now on, the diaper days are over. "Our own righteousness, measured by our efforts to keep the law, compares to filthy rags." Isaiah 64:6.)]

28 Nothing resembles your previous identity as Jew or Gentile, bond or free, male or female, now you are all defined in oneness with Christ. He is your significance and makes you beautiful.

[In Him the distinctions between Jew and Gentile, slave and free man, male and female, disappear; you are all one in Christ Jesus. (Weymouth Translation)]

29 Since Christ is the seed of promise, it is only in our realizing our union with him that we are equally related to Abraham and heirs of the promise. Faith and not flesh relates us to Abraham. (We inherit his righteousness by the same faith.) (MIRROR)

Galatians 4:

⁶ *To seal our sonship God has commissioned the Spirit of sonship to resonate the Abba echo in our hearts; and now, in our innermost being we recognize him as our true and very dear Father.*

Romans 8:

¹ *Now the decisive conclusion is this: in Christ, every bit of condemning evidence against us is canceled.*

² *The law of the Spirit is the liberating force of life in Christ. This leaves me with no further obligation to the law of sin and death. Spirit has superseded the sin enslaved senses as the principal law of our lives.*

(The law of the spirit is righteousness by faith versus the law of personal effort and self-righteousness which produces condemnation and spiritual death which is the fruit of the Do it yourself tree.)

³ *The law [of Moses] failed to be anything more than an instruction manual; it had no power to deliver us from the strong influence of sin holding us hostage in our own bodies. God disguised himself in his Son in this very domain where sin ruled us, in flesh.*

The body he lived and conquered in, was no different than ours.

Thus, sin's authority in the human body was condemned. (Hebrews 4:15, As High Priest he fully identifies with us in the context of our frail human life. Having subjected it to close scrutiny, he proved that the human frame was master over sin. His sympathy with us is not to be seen as excusing weaknesses that are the result of a faulty design, but rather as a trophy to mankind. He is not an example for us but of us.)

⁴ The very righteousness promoted by the law is now realized in us. Our practical day-to-day life bears witness to spirit inspiration and not flesh domination.

⁵ Sin's symptoms are sponsored by the senses, a mind dominated by the sensual. Thoughts betray source; spirit life attracts spirit thoughts.

⁶ Thinking patterns are formed by reference; either the sensual appetites of the flesh and spiritual death, or zoe-life and total tranquility flowing from a mind addicted to spirit [faith] realities.

⁷ A mind focused on flesh (the sensual domain where sin held us captive) is distracted from God with no inclination to his life-laws. Flesh [self-righteousness] and spirit [faith righteousness] are opposing forces. (Flesh no longer defines you; faith does.)

⁸ It is impossible for those immersed in flesh to at the same time accommodate themselves to the opinion, desire and interest of God.

⁹ But you are not ruled by flesh-consciousness, (law of works), but by spirit-consciousness [faith], since God's Spirit is permanently at home in you. Anyone who does not embrace the at-homeness of the Spirit of Christ, cannot be themselves.

¹⁰ The revelation of Christ in you declares that your body is as good as dead to sin's demands; sin cannot find any expression in a corpse. You co-died together with Him. Yet your spirit is alive because of what righteousness reveals.

¹¹ Our union with Christ further reveals that because the same Spirit who awakened the body of Jesus from the dead inhabits us, we equally participate in his resurrection. In this act of authority whereby God raised Jesus from the dead, He co-restores your body to life by his indwelling Spirit. (Your body need never again be an excuse for an inferior expression of the Christ-life, just as it was reckoned dead in Christ's death, it is now reckoned alive in his resurrection. ¹² We owe flesh nothing.

¹³ In the light of all this, to now continue to live under the sinful influences of the senses, is to reinstate the dominion of spiritual death. Instead, we are indebted to now exhibit the highest expression of life inspired by the Spirit. This life demonstrates zero tolerance to the habits and sinful patterns of the flesh.

[According to Romans 8:14, the original life of the Father revealed in his Son is the life the Spirit now conducts within us.]

¹⁵ Slavery is such a poor substitute for sonship. They are opposites; the one leads forcefully through fear; sonship responds fondly to Abba Father. His Spirit resonates within our spirit to confirm the fact that we originate in God.

¹⁶ Holy Spirit personally entwines our spirit; resonating ceaselessly within, endorsing Abba's parenthood.

[Because we are his offspring, we qualify to be his heirs, God himself is our portion, 17 we co-inherit with Christ.

Can you see how foolish it would be for a son to continue to live his life with a slave mentality? Your sonship qualifies you to immediately participate in all the wealth of God's inheritance which is yours because of Christ.

(Legalism in its every disguise contradicts sonship. Sonship is NOT FOR SALE!)] (MIRROR)

John 8:34 Jesus answered and said, "I say unto you with absolute certainty that everyone engaging in the distorted mindset of sin is a slave to it." (Sin is not about things you do or don't do—sin is missing out on sonship. (MIRROR)

For this reason, Paul wrote in Galatians 5:16:

I conclude: ***engage your spirit to be the dominant influence in your daily walk and see how it defeats the cravings of flesh.*** *(Spirit is satisfied by the love-law, the revelation of grace; flesh craves to prove and gratify itself by the DIY law. Faith defeats flesh.) (MIRROR) (Emphasis mine)*

Because our freedom to live from our spirit has been fully purchased, exemplified in Jesus, and made possible through the resurrection—sonship is our natural way of life now. We must begin to live *from* our spirit.

We bless our body and soul to be in their rightful place, not the dominant realm of our existence.

In 1 Thessalonians 5, we read:

[16] Be cheerfully happy at all times. [17] Constantly engage your thoughts in worshipful prayer. [18] Your gratitude is not based on anything fragile or

fading, but secured in the fact that God's purpose for you was concluded in Christ Jesus.

[19] Do not suffocate the flame of the Spirit within you. [20] The prophetic word is not to be underestimated. [21] Test everything like one would test gold to determine its true value, then treasure that which is precious with great care. [22] Distance yourselves immediately from every practice remotely related to the fruit of the "I-am-not-tree," which is the typical exhausting law of works system.

(The tree of the knowledge of good and evil represents mankind's lost sense of identity and righteousness, where mankind's global pursuit would now be their constant effort to achieve righteousness by means of their own works. This inevitably leads to disappointment, where shame replaces innocence, and union and fellowship are lost.

[23] There, away from any effort of your own, discover how the God of perfect peace, who fused you skillfully into oneness—just like a master craftsman would dovetail a carpentry joint—has personally perfected and sanctified the entire harmony of your being without your help. He has restored the detailed default settings. You were re-booted to fully participate in the life of your design, in your spirit, soul and body in blameless

innocence in the immediate presence of our Lord Jesus Christ.

[24] *You are defined by the faith of God; you are his poetry. (MIRROR)*

Chapter 4
The Kingdom Dynamic
of the Weapon of Patience

We found ourselves walking on a beautiful white marble floor with gold inlays. As we passed through large glass doors, we asked where we were. We heard a voice reply, "You're on my territory."

Not knowing who was speaking, the voice said, "Come this way. Follow my voice."

We were in what appeared to be a garden with a lot of mature trees in it.

The voice said, "You're getting closer."

We went around a bend and saw a cleft with a stream to the left of it. We could overlook a beautiful lush green valley with mountains behind it.

Stephanie remarked, "Whoever's territory this is, it's beautiful and lush."

She then saw a man with a burly beard. He had berries in his hand and was eating them. She said, "He's a big man in stature, and his beard is kind of wild."

Then she had a knowing that she was speaking to Bartholomew. "Are you Bartholomew from the Bible?" she asked.

He replied, "Why yes, I am."

Stephanie remarked, "Bartholomew, thank you for letting me be on your territory today. Can you share with us what Heaven has to say about it?"

He walked over to a bush that had berries on it and began eating the berries. He then walked over to a tree that looked like it had oranges. He plucked one from the tree and thrust his thumbs in it to open it up. Stephanie could smell the sweet aroma of the fruit. Bartholomew then walked over to a grove.

"Can you tell me what this is about?" Stephanie asked. "I'm very interested. I ask for Wisdom, Counsel, Knowledge and the Revelation Angel to be with my angels and me."

Bartholomew responded, "Don't worry, they're all here. This is for the Kingdom."

Stephanie replied, "Well, Bartholomew, your land and territory are lush. I know it is a representative of something. You have all this fruit. Is it fruits of the Spirit?"

Bartholomew remarked, "It is the good gift of the Father. I'm able to enjoy harvest, even here. I'm here to offer fruit."

Bartholomew asked, "What are the fruits of the spirit?"

Stephanie answered, "Well, there's peace, love, joy, gentleness, longsuffering, kindness, goodness, mercy, and self-control."

Bartholomew inquired, "What else is fruit? Time is fruit. What are you willing to sow to reap?"

Stephanie replied, "I am willing to sow time. I'm willing to sow the gifts the Father has given me into others' lives. I'm willing to sow faith."

Bartholomew responded, "Those are all really good things."

Bartholomew asked, "Are you willing to sow patience? To you, what is patience?"

Stephanie remarked, "Well, it's a lot of things to me. What is it to Heaven?"

Bartholomew explained, "That's the right question. Patience is exactly what you did. When you dropped your sword,[2] you were willing to wait. You were ready to lay down your desires and your wants, and if you think

---

[2] Bartholomew was aware of an engagement earlier that morning when Stephanie purposely laid down her sword to allow the Lord to fight a battle for her.

about it, Stephanie, you weren't even desperate. You just knew you weren't going to fight, and you were going to let it be the Lord's battle. That's what patience is. When you patiently waited, the answer came quickly.

In order for the sons to have victory, they need to son in patience.

Sons need to rule from patience. There is great victory in patience.

This isn't just being patient with a loved one; this is patiently waiting on God's hand to move and show the victory. But is it a laying down? Did you not have to lay something down?"

Stephanie replied, "I did. I laid down my sword; I laid down the fight. I didn't want it. I felt like I was stuck again."

Bartholomew said, "You were not stuck. You just exercised patience."

Bartholomew asked, "Why do you think the sons struggle with patience?"

Stephanie responded, "Well, my question back to you, Bartholomew is, hasn't it always been that way because we are a generation where instantaneously we have things?"

Bartholomew replied, "Indeed, it always has been."

We began walking through his territory and took it in.

Bartholomew said, "All of these things that are here—this harvest is here because I had to learn patience. There is a great harvest in walking in patience. The fight truly is the Lord's. I had to lay down my desires and my wants and say to the Lord; I am not fighting this battle. It's not mine to fight. And besides that, it is already won. This is strategic. It's a strategy. This comes from the strategy room. It can be sought after."

Stephanie said, "Are you saying that this kind of patience we're talking about is like a weapon?"

Bartholomew replied, "It *IS* a weapon. The defeat is mighty. What did you see on the table when you laid your sword down in the exchange room?"

Stephanie responded, "I saw the defeated carcasses of my enemies."

Bartholomew asked, "Well, who are *your* enemies?"

Stephanie remarked, "They are the Lord's enemies."

Bartholomew continued, "Walk with me. Do you know that there is much knowledge to be gained? Can you be patient?"

The Challenge of Striving

Stephanie asked, "This is about striving, isn't it? People have been striving and striving, going through all this information and knowledge. They can lay that down, just like the sword, and you just showed me that the answers come faster when you do that.

Father, where I have strived out of my flesh, I repent and ask for the blood of Jesus to cover it.

I lay that striving down upon the table in exchange for what you have. I'm not going to fight this battle; it is futile.

Stephanie described what she saw, "I saw myself laying down the sword and striving onto the table. The word that came back was 'multiplicity.' It's literally a giant word on this table. Bartholomew is in this room with me. We at once were out of his territory and in this room—an exchange room."

The Kingdom Principle of Patience

"May I ask, Bartholomew, why you are here today?"

Bartholomew said, "I'm trading. I struggled with patience when I was on earth. *But once I learned the Kingdom principle of patience, things multiplied and came faster.*"

Bartholomew walked toward the double doors, opened them, and threw a handful of berries he had into the back of his mouth, smiled, turned away, and walked out. He was enjoying his harvest.

———·———

Chapter 5
The Kingdom Dynamic of Being Uncompromised

As we engaged Heaven this day, a man in white named Gabriel came to guide us. We were in a palace and began walking down a massive hallway. It was wide with a red carpet.

There was artwork on the walls, which were decorated with immense portraits that were tall—from floor to ceiling and the ceiling seemed to be 50 to 75 feet tall. He explained that we were in the palace of the king and told us to enjoy the scenery.

It was all quite exquisite, and two very large wooden doors were in front of us. It was made of beautiful wood and had a curve around the top of it. Gabriel pulled the handles on it, and it opened to a banquet hall. There were many people in the banquet hall, and they were eating and drinking. Gabriel redirected us through this large room, through a smaller doorway and into a smaller hallway. The sign above the door read, "The King's Court."

It felt more personal, not like an actual courtroom, but a private office. We sat down, and Stephanie was handed the book of Psalms. She had seen this book before and noted the stains from teardrops on some of the pages.

Initially, we thought it was Jesus' Palace, the palace of the King, but this was David's Palace—the Palace of the king. David was not in the room, so we asked where to look in the book we held. We were told to look at Psalm 37 (in The Passion Translation). It was a song of wisdom. We were pointed to verse 3:

---

*Keep trusting in the Lord
and do what is right in His eyes.
Fix your heart on the promises of God
and you will be secure,
feasting on His faithfulness.*

King David came in wearing hunting gear. A revelation about hunting in Heaven came that one does not hunt to kill but simply as a game. David was hunting, and they were hunting him at the same time.

David put a large sword on the desk, picked up a duplicate of the book we had, and mentioned the tears that had stained some of the pages. He asked if we thought the tears came from anguish and pain, which we had surmised, but he pointed out that just as many tears of joy were shed.

He told us to be uncompromised. He repeated it several times.

We were impressed to look at Psalm 102. The title was, "From Tears to Praise."

In this Psalm the tears were of anguish at the beginning but ended in tears of joy and praise. We then were directed to Psalm 55 where the last phrase was "You'll never fail to rescue me." Again, he reiterated that we be uncompromised.

Keeping our spirit forward keeps us from being compromised in all things.

Having our spirit lead will prevent us from compromising. To do so, we must have one foot in the realm of Heaven and one foot upon the earth. To do this, we must:

- Call our spirit forward.
- Step into the realms of Heaven.
- Call for the Glory to stand up within us.
- Step into the Spirit of Excellence.

We are more sensitive to the things of the spirit when we step in. We can do that all day—every day, even as we walk out our steps upon our path on the earth. This is a Kingdom Dynamic principle.

---
*Being uncompromised is
a Kingdom dynamic principle.*

At times David did compromise but...

---
*When David was with the Father,
and was in tune with Him,
He was never compromised.*

With those comments, our engagement with David was over. We then got up and walked out of David's Palace with Gabriel, our guide.

———·———

Chapter 6
The Kingdom Dynamic of Possessing Your Mountaintop

As we engaged Heaven, we found ourselves on a mountain. It wasn't a large mountain, but it was snow-capped. Asking where we were and what it meant, the question came, "Where does revelation put man?"

According to this vision, we replied that it would put us on a mountaintop. Our tutor then asked if we thought there were any valleys in revelation. Of course, we could not see any valleys.

Our tutor rephrased the question and asked if there were highs and lows in revelation. We had no answer and requested that our tutor tell us.

We stood on top of a mountain in the engagement with our feet firmly planted.

With revelation, your feet are planted firmly on solid ground.

If the sons could see themselves from this point of view, they could conquer much. They would conquer everything because there are no obstructions. Everything is small in perspective.

If our feet are planted on solid ground, lifted high, and elevated as in this picture, why would the sons not choose to see themselves here moment by moment and day by day?

Fear would be a culprit. One of the strategies of hell has been to plant people's feet lower beneath the revelation of Jesus.

---

*The fact that you are sons—
see yourself elevated higher.*

The word says, "He is high and lifted up."[3] So are his sons.

---

*Plant your feet on the solid ground
that is revelation.*

In our times of wanting, we must rule from this place by using the imagination of our hearts and see our feet on this mountain that is revelation, that we are sons and there are no obstructions in our way.

---

[3] Isaiah 6:1

It is much easier when you rule from revelation than from the valley.

Paul understood this from the revelation he received from Heaven.[4] He trusted the revelation as having come from Heaven and once he leaned into it, he understood it. Once he understood it, he could rule as a son despite the persecution. The persecution was not the problem. The problem would have been not ruling as a son, high up on the mountain of revelation. It is the only way he survived.

We can learn to use this knowledge in a timelier manner by stepping into the Court of Times and Seasons and going ahead of time. In the realms of Heaven, time is not a limitation like it is on the earth. In Heaven, tomorrow is as close as next year, or the next decade or century. As we step into Heaven we step outside the restraints of time and can go where we need to go, forward or backwards.

Heaven wants us to understand ruling from the mountaintop of revelation so we can rule in the mountains assigned to us. Each of us has a mountain—a place to rule from in some arena whether it is business, family, religion, entertainment, or another mountain of culture. Some mountains still have no one ruling upon them.

---

[4] Paul's time in Arabia was spent receiving and activating revelation in his life.

Rule from Your Mountaintop

Ezekiel Building Steps

The next vision was of Ezekiel and his troops carving out staircases for easier access to people's mountaintops. They were assisting. We commissioned him saying,

We commission you to prepare and make a more accessible pathway for the people of LifeSpring, those who draw near, and their families to the access points. Remove all obstacles as they journey to their mountaintop of revelation in Jesus' name.

Father, I ask on behalf of Ezekiel, his ranks, and his commanders for the tools needed to carve out and remove the debris along the way of people's access points to their revelation that they may set their feet on the solid ground at the top.

We commend Ezekiel, his commanders, ranks and patrollers to you, Father. And we ask for angel food, angel bread, and angel elixir to be given to them.

Father, I asked for the sickle for Ezekiel, his commanders, and ranks to remove and cut through the mountains that are in the way of the people in Jesus' name.

The view from the mountaintop is extraordinary. The air is cleaner. It is quieter. Moses would often go to the mountaintop to receive from Heaven. Many who are drawn to LifeSpring are either on their mountain or climbing it. Some are still on the journey, but they are close.

———·———

Chapter 7
The Kingdom Dynamic of Trusting Your Spirit

As we engaged Heaven, we saw George carving a piece of soapstone. We wondered what the lesson with the soapstone was. He had yet to receive specific instructions before he began carving. His spirit knew how to do it.

Many people say they don't trust themselves. They may trust their soul, but what about trusting your spirit? George's spirit man knew how to carve the soapstone and had already been instructed by the Lord in how to do it.

How do we trust our spirit?

First, we need to realize that our spirit man is whole and complete and has Holy Spirit residing within it. Our spirit is what the Father sees when he sees us. That is how he sees the righteousness of Jesus upon us. It is on our spirit. Because of that, we can trust our spirit.

We are learning to call our spirits forward. When calling your spirit forward, instruct it to do the things our Father does. That is how Jesus was able to say to his disciples that He does the things His Father does because it was His spirit doing them. That is how we can separate the man from the Christ.

After we have called our spirits forward, the next step is having our spirit interact with things. This is the next step.

We want to walk on water, don't we? Of course, we do.

When our spirit leads, the result will be a masterpiece because the Lord has already taught us. How else, or what else will we know that the Lord has taught our spirit man?

We are in a time and a season of revelation. Many will walk in knowledge that the Lord has instructed them within their spirit. This is truly a trust about trust.

This is why we learned about trusts first: get them cleaned up and cleaned out and get the gates of hell away, so we can have our trust. It's twofold. We trust in Father, and what He's doing with our spirit. It's our trust, which is our inheritance. There is an order to it. There will be things to do that our soul and mind have no idea how to accomplish.

I first experienced this years ago when I owned a computer company. I would troubleshoot and repair issues on our client's computer systems. I had never taken any computer courses, and I did not own a computer for the first two years. I simply relied on Holy Spirit. He would show me what to do through words of wisdom or words of knowledge, and the problem would be solved. This happened over and over in the fifteen years I was in that business while also pastoring churches.

In these times, we are going to be worshiping in spirit and in truth. There will be things our spirit man will automatically know how to do that are different from what our mind and soul knows how to do. Let us learn to flow with the instruction of Heaven and trust our spirit.

———·———

Chapter 8
The Kingdom Dynamic of Walking on Water

Peter appeared to us in an engagement with Heaven (the one who walked on water) and had come to explain the dynamics of how he could do so.

Peter walked in the strength that came from the adjudication.[5] In our weakness, *He* is strong, especially in the court processes. This is where we lean not upon our own understanding. If we remain in that humility, we will bear much fruit.

It seemed as if Peter had joined our team in our engagements with Heaven. He handed us a scroll. We opened it and read the phrase "Next Steps." He began teaching us about governing, specifically lessons that he

---

[5] Adjudication is the process of performing court work on a situation resulting in a verdict being granted.

had learned the hard way. He wanted to bring ease to us in learning to govern.

---

*Governing is not just a tool,
it is a right.*

It's where there is strength and adjudication. The perception has been that a person is too weak in their understanding to go into the courts. It is not in their strength. If they could go into the courts with the mindset of where they are weak, He is strong; then *there will be strength in the adjudication process for each person.* It is the truth.

---

*Heaven wants us to come out
of old mindsets.*

This is not in and of ourselves. Lean on Counsel, lean on Wisdom."[6]

Peter struggled with this. Even though he walked with Jesus, he thought he knew everything. He learned differently as part of his journey.

While engaging with Peter in Heaven, Peter said, "Revelation will be coming at lightning speed in the times ahead, yet the Father never gives us more than we can handle."

---

[6] Wisdom and Counsel are entities in the realms of Heaven with whom we can engage and receive revelation and insight from.

Peter, who walked on water,[7] then began walking on water. Peter was the one that got out of the boat, and he has always been razzed for sinking in the water, while everyone else was safely in the boat.

Heaven wants us to know we can do this too.

Jesus said we would do these things and greater.[8] We have believed it in our head but not necessarily in our hearts.

The reason Peter sank was that he got all up in his head.

Walking on water
is not head knowledge.
It never can be.
Everything is a spiritual matter.

When I say 'matter,' we must consider the matter that the water is made of compared to the matter that makes up our bodies. Our bodies are weightier and will sink. But...

If we were spirit-forward,
our spirit would carry our body.

---

[7] Matthew 14:25-32
[8] John 14:12

As our spirit comes forward, it becomes like a bubble that encapsulates our body enabling it to float.

When Jesus called Peter onto the water, his spirit man *was* forward. He was excited realizing it was Jesus on the water and that Jesus had invited him to join Him—the one he loved—his brother—the one he believed in so much. Before he even realized what he was doing, he was out of the boat and on the water. Then, he got into his head, his spirit man took a back seat, and his soul came forward. That's why he began to sink. Don't get me wrong; He believed in the principle of being spirit-forward.

---

*Live spirit-forward
and we will walk on water.*

Chapter 9
The Kingdom Dynamic of Strength & Adjudication

We had been engaging Heaven with Lydia and noticed that she seemed more illuminated than before. She pointed out that men and women in white can adjust their frequency and brightness, just like the angels. However, in this engagement, she explained that she had not increased her brightness but that the entity of LifeSpring was in a new place with Heaven and its illumination had been turned up. It was about our vision—our new spectacles. Because of that, we could see the Glory of God on things.

We knew we needed strength for what we were about to learn. The woman in white behind the Help Desk then pushed a file across the desk on which was printed the word "adjudication."

It was explained to us that there is strength in the adjudication of the court cases we're bringing because of the level we've come to. This is the court's recognition of the work we and our team had been doing."

LifeSpring was viewed as a strength in the court for everybody coming near the ministry.

There has been a strength. We have been receiving a shoring up and a greater understanding in the courts of our strength as the entity of LifeSpring International Ministries. This includes those working on behalf of LifeSpring and those learning this.

We were brought into a court scenario and watched the judge and someone else in front of him. The person was a newbie at working in the courts, but the strength in their willingness to learn and sit under the teaching of LifeSpring has strengthened their case. The court views this willingness as a strengthening of the adjudication.

We humbly submit that it is because of wisdom, knowledge, understanding, and the Father's love and strengthening of us. There is a strength in the corporate body coming together with court cases. An example was a recent series of court cases involving Canada that Heaven said we played a part in the successful outcome of those cases.

Strength is in the corporate court cases. Periodically during Sandhills Ecclesia, we will conduct court cases as an ecclesia. It strengthens the participants when we do so. They will find strength and freedom from them—not only for them but also for their generations.

> *When we bring court cases as an ecclesia, it builds unity among the body.*

The corporate anointing has a strength to it that we are learning to work with.

———·———

Chapter 10
The Kingdom Dynamic of a Molecular Walk

Stephanie opened our engagement by hearing the phrase "lease agreement." We asked for understanding, but she found herself walking on water before it came. It was in a shallow brook, but she was on the water. She could feel her feet getting wet, but there was a slight distance between the top of the water and the bottom of her foot—about ¼ inch. She could not feel the rocks underneath her feet as you usually would if walking through a small brook.

She was wondered what was happening when she saw Timothy at the top of the bank overlooking the brook. He asked if she enjoyed walking on water.

Of course, she did and noted her surprise at being able to do so. Timothy remarked that everyone who experienced that was also surprised the first time they did it. He motioned for her to come up the embankment, and once she did, she found herself walking on top of the grass—not touching it, but her feet were just slightly above the tips of the blades of grass. It was similar to her experience of walking on water. The lesson was about the molecular properties of her, the water, and the grass. We were to learn a little about the governing of the molecular.

We watched as he instructed a tree to move. He placed his hand on it, and it moved over slightly.

Timothy remarked that as the spirit leads, the rest will follow.

As our spirit leads, we begin to govern. There is no formula. The connectivity between our molecular being and what we are governing is molecular. It is an agreement.

There was a play on words with what he just said, "As the spirit leads, the rest will follow." The spirit will lead us into rest. And rest is where we do these things of which he is speaking. It will be done with ease.

Acts of agreement are molecular.

Our molecular being must agree with the molecular properties of that which we seek to govern.

When we do that, we will understand that we are as light as a feather as we walk on water and that the grass understands that we are as light as a feather as we walk on it.

Why does Heaven want us to walk on water?

> *Heaven wants us to govern every environment.*

> *Heaven wants us to govern cross-dimensionally.*

It is not just where we learn how to walk with one foot in Heaven and one foot on earth, but we do this in more than one dimension.

> *We are sons—govern.*

Timothy then walked inside the tree and disappeared.

Chapter 11
The Kingdom Dynamic of Your Lease Agreement

We then asked Malcolm to draw near, hoping he would help us understand what was meant by the phrase "lease agreement" mentioned in the previous chapter.

He appeared with a Lease Agreement in his hand. We asked him to explain. If all of this (speaking of the world around us) belongs to the Father, how would we feel if we knew that the Father is leasing it out to us to govern it?

Every lease has conditions.

When you have a lease agreement in the natural, you may have full rights to the property as long as you maintain the conditions of the lease. The children of Israel were given a lease to the lands they possessed. Their part of maintaining the lease conditions was not to cohabitate and mix with other races, not serve other gods, and things like that. They broke the agreement, and as a result, they lost the land.

Malcom held the lease agreement in his hand to show us that we must govern properly. When we govern from this understanding, the lease is intact.

Govern what you have been given.

Have we been given everything because we are sons of the Father? Who owns the cattle on a thousand hills?

Just as in the Parable of the Talents, when the master gave sums of money to his servants, the lesson was about governing and the costs of governing properly or improperly.

---
*If we govern our territory
and what we have in front of us,
WE WILL BE GIVEN MORE!
It will expand!*

We have seen that with LifeSpring. He has given us much more territory. The image of the lease agreement was for the sake of visualizing it and our responsibility to it.

Malcolm asked Stephanie if she would like to have a lease agreement that was enacted today?

Of course, she did. Malcolm then showed her where she had already signed it—before time. He explained that the agreement for today is for our eyes of understanding that this has already been done.

Stephanie declared,

I say 'yes' to the lease agreement, Father. I thank You that You were with me in the beginning when I signed it originally. You were with each of us when we signed ours.

Help us to expand, to govern properly, as sons, and to be able to share this in a manner with which people can visually understand it, see it, and know it for themselves.

Father, forgive me for not taking my lease agreement and stewarding it correctly. I repent and ask for the blood of Jesus to cover that sin.

In Isaiah 54:2, we read:

Enlarge the place of your tent and let them stretch out the curtains of your habitation; spare not, lengthen your cords and strengthen your stakes. For you shall spread out to the right hand and to the left, and your descendants shall inherit the nations and make the desolate cities to be inhabited.

Much of what we do is a matter of stewardship. If you want your territory to grow, govern well. We will learn more about this principle as we continue through this book.

Happy governing!

———·———

Chapter 12

The Kingdom Dynamic of Considering the Stars

As we engaged Heaven, we found ourselves standing behind Ezekiel, our ministry angel. He turned to us and said, "Consider the stars."

We were looking at an enormous star and were watching it change colors. It changed from a beautiful red to a golden color to a bluish purple.

We asked, "What's happening with this star? How do we consider the stars?"

Ezekiel replied, "All of creation is groaning for the sons of men to take their place. SPEAK."

Stephanie remarked, "He wants me to speak to it. Ezekiel, what do I speak specifically?"

Ezekiel explained, "Speak the name above all names."

Stephanie responded, "I speak Jesus. I also speak YHWH."

When she said both of those names, from inside of the star light came out. Light beams come from all around it.

Ezekiel said, "You are the light in the world. He is the light of the world. This is a navigation point. Consider the stars."

Stephanie remarked, "There's a Scripture we're supposed to understand around consider the stars. Ezekiel, can you help me know what Scripture reference you want us to speak to the star?"

Ezekiel replied, "This is about speaking the word, the word doesn't return void.[9]"

Psalm 8:3-4 came to mind:

³ Look at the splendor of your skies, your creative genius glowing in the heavens. When I gaze at your moon and your stars, mounted like jewels in their settings, I know you are the fascinating artist who fashioned it all! But when I look up and see such wonder and workmanship above, I have to ask you this question: ⁴ Compared to all this cosmic glory, why would you bother with puny, mortal man or be infatuated with Adam's sons? (TPT)

---

[9] Isaiah 55:11 So shall My word be that goes forth from My mouth; It shall not return to Me void, But it shall accomplish what I please, And it shall prosper in the thing for which I sent it.

Ezekiel confirmed that Psalm 8:3-4 was the Scripture he was referring to.

He said, "Read the next Scripture because it's the answer to; why would you bother with puny mortal men."

Psalms 8:5-6:

⁵ Yet what honor you have given to men, created only a little lower than Elohim, crowned like kings and queens with glory and magnificence.

⁶ You have delegated to them mastery over all you have made, making everything subservient to their authority, placing earth itself under the feet of your image-bearers. (TPT)

Ezekiel said, "Stop right there. The earth itself is under your feet.

You have stars, and the sons of men are to govern the stars.

"This is placement! This is the understanding of placement and order."

Take your rightful place!

With that, Ezekiel flew off and our engagement ended.

Chapter 13
The Kingdom Dynamic of Sacred Ground

As we began this engagement, we found ourselves walking through a battlefield strewn with carcasses of beasts of all sorts. Ezekiel, his commanders, and ranks were busy cleaning the ground. He explained that what we saw was the aftermath of a battle. The enemy had crossed over sacred ground and had been thoroughly defeated.

This was sacred ground, and these beasts had been trespassing.

Sacred grounds are things that have been deeded over to the Lord.

This is what it looks like when the sons of men are armored up, and they trample the enemy underfoot. Imagine what it will look like when we fully use our star.

We are just learning about our stars and already seeing outcomes. This was a result. This was the trampling underfoot—a result of governing the earth that belongs to Him and the sons.

The Lord is always at work on behalf of the sons—the unity, and their coming together.

The governing of the territory produces results like this.

This is a type of pushback. We could tell that Ezekiel had been enjoying himself immensely. The sons are awakening because this work is what the angels are built to do.

Of course, the angels need refreshing after a battle, so we made a request.

Father, we ask for refreshing for Ezekiel, his commanders, and ranks.

We request angel food, bread, and elixir of every color and number.

We request the kind of shoes he needs.

(He was walking away, and I was able to focus on his shoes.)

We request, Father, the shoes for Ezekiel to tread on the enemy.

We are asking for the expansion that Ezekiel needs with his commanders and ranks.

This is dimensional work. It differs from the standard work many of us have been accustomed to doing.

——— · ———

Chapter 14
The Kingdom Dynamic
of Dimensional Work

We had just concluded the prior engagement when our faithful tutor Malcolm appeared. The dimensional shift that had just occurred gave the sense that Stephanie was standing in the middle of a piece of glass. She could see below, but there wasn't anything directly underneath her. However, there were several triangular doorways around her. There was nothing directly above her either, only that which was in front of her and up high and down low. She was in the middle.

It was a starting point. It was where she could choose which dimension to go in. It was a jumping-off place. She was standing on something that looked like glass. About ten feet around her were triangular doorways. There was a level above her, and a level above that one, and it kept going. However, there was nothing directly above her head.

Then, she could see the same thing below her, with each level below it and more levels below that. She could choose any door. She could turn around and see inside each door, but there was a different scene in each. She could barely see the scenery because of so many doors, but she could see there was scenery in each one. It was an interesting picture of what a dimensional paradox is.

This is where we will ask to be led by Wisdom into these dimensional places. There are so many. We should be thankful to be led by Wisdom at every turn. Heaven uses the phrase "at every turn," because we can turn and see all these places available to us to walk in. We will need Wisdom to know which door to walk through.

Wisdom showed me how this would work. We will feel a pull towards one of these open doors. I would be happy with Wisdom if she would just stick me right through a door of her choosing. That's not how this is going to work. We will be able to choose. Therefore, invoke Wisdom at every turn.

My Territory

Wisdom suggested that Stephanie go see her territory. She agreed and immediately found herself at a door. She could see the landscape. She hadn't gone through the door yet, but could see through it. It was as if the door was open, and she could stick her head through the doorway and view the landscape.

She could see angels or men or women in white building something on her land—structures. They were starting on the spiritual foundations.

She saw another door and peeked through, where she saw an old garden. Wisdom reminded her that she had been to that place before. It was one she had seen when she was in her twenties.

Stephanie's Vision

Stephanie shared:

I had a vision when I was in my twenties. I was in and out of sleep. I had been asking the Lord to let me know about my biological father. I wanted to know if he was in Heaven or not, I knew nothing about that side of my family. For whatever reason, and for about a month, I was burdened with whether he was saved. I never knew him, so I didn't care before, but this was so strong in my heart. I finally said, either tell me or take this feeling from me because there's not anything I can do about it one way or the other; he's already dead.

Then this vision came. I was standing in the back end of a garden. There was a white picket fence. There were flowers everywhere. In front of me, in part of the fencing, was an opening somebody would have to walk through to enter this garden. The garden looked young, but the sun was bright as I looked in that direction. I saw somebody walking toward me, and I thought it might be Jesus because the closer the person got, I began to feel this overwhelming, tangible love. It started in my chest, and the closer this person got, the bigger this tangible feeling got. The person that came was my dad. He spoke to me and told me lots and lots of things.

We will need Wisdom, and we will need to invoke her at every turn regarding dimensional work. It's all very scientific—it's quantum.

———·———

Chapter 15
The Kingdom Dynamic of Exchange

In an earlier engagement with Heaven, Stephanie laid down her sword to signify she was allowing the Lord to fight her battle. Ezekiel came and brought her the sword she had laid down. He indicated that she had many swords, not just one.

We were now in the realms of Heaven, and on the countertop of the Help Desk lay a yellow envelope. Stephanie turned it over and opened it. It contained two passes on lanyards that we were to wear.

The woman at the Help Desk led us down the hallway. We entered the first room on the right. In the middle of the room were two floor-to-ceiling columns. The room was like a conference room. Walking around the columns to get a better view, we saw that the room was built with gold bricks. The entire room had elements of gold throughout. I could see the walls were not solid gold, but a layer of gold was in the middle of them. We were in an exchange room.

Wondering what we were to exchange in that room, Stephanie was instructed to take the sword she had dropped and put it on the table.

As soon as she placed the sword on the table, it changed to something else. We discovered that when you put something on the table, it is replaced with something better—it transforms immediately.

We could not yet get a clear picture of all that was on the table, but we saw that the sword had multiplied. The one sword became a pile of swords approximately three feet high, and there were other things piled on top of one another.

We were viewing a hologram of all the things that had been defeated. It was like the carcasses we had seen before with Ezekiel, but these were bags of defeated carcasses piled on top of one another. We were grateful but also interested in how this was an exchange.

Ezekiel showed us that when Stephanie dropped that particular sword, it was because she had said to the Lord, "You must fight my battles. Therefore, I put my sword down."

Stephanie could not fight her own battles nor wanted to, so she made an exchange.

At first, she thought that dropping her sword and then having Ezekiel return it to her meant she had done something wrong, but that's not what it was at all. She had put her sword down. She had said, "No, I'm dropping my sword here. I'm not fighting this battle."

As we were in this Exchange Room, we wondered what else we could place on this table. We realized we could put anything on it.

I was impressed to asked her, "Is there something in your hands or pockets?"

Stephanie laughed and said, "I don't know why, but I have marbles in my pockets."

I instructed her, "Lay them on the table."

She laid them on the table, and instantly, they grew in size and became pieces of a territory. She could see the spheres and could look inside of each of them. She could see water and land. Inside one was gold. There were many different spheres.

She asked, "How do I take these with me? I've had them in my pockets, and I didn't even mean to. I want to take these and give them to the Lord, or how does this work?"

Having been instructed to walk around the table, she noticed one of the spheres was extremely bright. She could not see a landscape or anything inside it, but she was instructed to place her entire face into it to view it. As she did, she recognized that these were her territories and landscapes, but they were in different dimensions.

Ezekiel pulled it off the table and placed it in front of her. It was now as tall as her and still round in shape. She stepped into it. She could see someone on the other side so she tapped them on the shoulder and greeted them. She did not recognize them. She asked Wisdom to come alongside to assist her. Wisdom immediately came with a host of angels.

We were asked if we wanted every dry place deeded and given to the Lord so the only steward would be us and the Father. Of course, we replied affirmatively, and although we may have prayed a similar prayer before, Heaven reminded us that this is dimensional work. Therefore, it is helpful to add a phrase to a request like, "I ask this be done in time and out of time, and in every realm and dimension, in Jesus' name.

We all have dimensions and places that haven't been deeded yet. These are places we have never been. It is undiscovered territory and landscape. It is undiscovered revelation. It is undiscovered opportunities and undiscovered resources. We are explorers. We are in the process of mapping out these places.

When explorers were discovering the world, they would map out parts of the territories found. This is a spiritual mapping out. These are undiscovered inheritances. Some have been ruled by entities that pollute the territory.

When we discover new territory with occupants, we need to remove them if Heaven has not assigned them to the land.

Wisdom showed us to do this:

Father, every territory that is mine, in every dimension, in every paradigm, in every place that is undiscovered resources, inheritances, regions and places in quantum, [which to me also means ahead of time, behind time, in every realm and dimension and every timeline].

I deed everything over to you. I want the removal of all entities and deities that have claimed my territories. I haven't authorized them to be there, and don't agree with it. I want the immediate removal of all entities at any dry place or any discovered place, in Jesus' name.

I'm handing all the deeds to you, Father, because I don't want them. I want you to have them. Help me to steward them correctly.

Stephanie had sensed someone on this territory, found herself in front of the person, and realized it was a fractured part of a lingering human spirit. The enemy takes fractured pieces and puts them on territories that are other people. This is not unlike how LHS's are assigned to our body, soul, and spirit realms.

Wisdom showed us how to take care of this so that every piece of a person's parts are brought back to him.

Father, I ask to step into the Mercy Court on behalf of this person, where a part of him has been in this place for a long time.

Father, there has been false worship. This person was told to worship other gods and deities and he made sacrifices to them. He was broken and fractured in many ways because during his life he sold out to these other deities.

Father, I repent on his behalf and behalf of his generations for all of the egregious sins that were ever committed, those that he committed, or his family committed. I repent for the sin of profane worship of every kind in Jesus' name.

We also want to know if there are fractures on territories that belong to me.

The enemy does this to everybody throughout their generational line as far as sin is concerned. There is nothing new under the sun.

Stephanie continued:

Father, for all that has been repented of on his behalf and on behalf of his family, I ask for the blood of Jesus, and I asked for angels to go and retrieve all of his parts from every place, in every dimension, and every realm.

I commission them to retrieve them from territory that belongs to me or anyone else and bring him back whole.

She watched as layers of him came back to him. To be sure the work was complete, she asked Wisdom if all of his parts were compiled. Stephanie sensed they were, so she declared, "From this place, I'm going to govern."

She then opened the silver channel and had the angels assist the LHS in stepping into Heaven. Stephanie dealt with the principality and with the demonic guards and closed the silver channel in the name of Jesus. She then requested a sweeping of all of the spiritual debris and that it be done in every realm. She asked that it be done on every piece of territory and on every undiscovered inheritance that had been deeded to the Lord and to do it quantumly.

The lesson is to exchange all your territory, all your inheritance, and all of your resources. Exchange it with the Father; He will reveal what you need to know. Here the Father is handing us something, and we're handing it back to him. Just like when we are crowned, we give our crowns back. What is happening is, He turns around and gives it back to us again in return and it is multiplied. That is where we started—the exchange.

Stephanie prayed:

I take all my territories, future resources, and everything that the Father has given me, and I lay them on the table and deed everything to Him.

In return, He is giving us more revelation for LHS's. It's as if the redeeming of territory and landscape for us redeems other people too. He is always redeeming.

Wisdom, we exchange our inheritance. We've been talking about stepping into our inheritance as sons, but we turn around and give it back. It's a constant exchange back and forth.

Father, this is Your inheritance You give to us. We give it back to You.

It's a constant growing of our inheritance, back and forth.

The Father is always redeeming other sons. Since the beginning of time, the enemy has taken men and women captive in more than just natural ways. He has taken captive their hearts, fractured their minds, and placed them in places he (the enemy) deemed undiscoverable. But as you know, light exposes the darkness.

The remedy to everything is love. He loves. He is redeeming His sons—those who are fractured LHS's, in those undiscoverable places. The Father wants us to know they are discovered and have always been revealed to Heaven.

Now, as sons, we work in tandem as we deed our territories, lands, and inheritances to the Lord. His promises are 'yes and amen' to those put in darkness, whose parts are in undiscovered places.

Look what the Lord has done. What the enemy sought to be harm; the Lord has redeemed. He has redeemed the sons.

As we walk in paradigms of prayer, Father is also giving fractured parts of others full redemption. Wisdom showed us that even though thousands of years ago (that's what the person Stephanie sensed earlier felt like to her), a fractured part of an LHS was put in a place (undiscovered territory) that the enemy thought was undiscoverable. The enemy put these LHS's fractured parts on a territory that belonged to a son who was going to come into this revelation. That son would be able to redeem another (an LHS) through the process of deeding all their own territory over to the Lord. The enemy cannot win.

How does the enemy know where all these dimensions and places are? Think of all the fragmented parts of LHS's that are on people's territories, polluting them. Most have no idea that there is a defilement on their land/territory.

What is challenging about redemption?

The world is going to have full knowledge of lingering human spirits. There will be so much cleanup work that people will be doing with this knowledge in three years' time.

There will often be trades to hinder your walk where you don't know where to look. This information will be in the Guest Registry. Everything is in the Guest Registry if we know what to look for.

Now we can look in the registry and ask if there are any LHS's on different territories, in different dimensions and paradigms, or are there fractured parts? And on what territories? And do these territories belong to other people? Their presence is a pollution of that realm. That's where we go next.

> *From this realm that I still see we just removed the LHS from, I govern it in the name of Jesus. I call in living water.*
>
> *I call in the scrolls for this territory and I call in for the scroll to be planted in the ground as seed on this territory, for it to be watered by the blood and living water.*
>
> *I commission angels to steward this land and this territory, in this dimension, in this paradigm in Jesus' name."*

She then saw a whirlwind. It looked like rain, and it was watering that realm or territory. It had felt so dry and now she was watching it being watered.

She remarked, "Wisdom, we have two lessons about paradigms and realms, don't we? The first lesson is about exchanging, and the second is looking for fractured parts and LHS's on territories in the Guest Registry.

What is so interesting is the clear picture of the Lord allowing the enemy to put a fractured part on a son's territory who is going to realize and do this redemptive work. That son is going to find these LHS's. The sons will learn these lessons about LHS's, and fractured parts. The sons will know how and learn how to govern and will do this work to set many free. It's so fitting that the Lord is constantly redeeming us and others at the same time while making the enemy look foolish. The enemy has been outdone again.

I recommended Stephanie check her pockets a second time. She did and discovered an envelope. Instead of opening the envelope, she placed it on the table in exchange. A giant tree grew in front of her, full of fruit. It was not the Tree of the Knowledge of Good and Evil. It was filled with letters and envelopes, hanging all over the tree for us to explore.

She took one and opened it and found a love letter addressed to the "Crowned one."

I then suggested she check her back pocket. She did and discovered a watch. She laid it on the Exchange Table and immediately was taken into a wormhole—a tunnel. When she came out the other side, she saw Jesus walking toward her in sandals and a white tunic.

He had some more things to teach us. He started saying that all He is asking is for us to exchange these things with Him, and He will multiply. He will give back to us pressed down, running over. It is a constant exchange. When we give something to Jesus, he returns it multiplied. It is never given in an exact exchange, nor do we ever receive less than what we have given. We give our hearing, seeing, knowledge, wisdom, and our understanding. We give it all to Him. Jesus reminded us that all He has He has given to us. We must learn to steward well what He has given.

The watch she found symbolized time that had been stolen from her. She exchanged it for the restoration of time in her life. Jesus suddenly disappeared and Stephanie could see the wormhole again. She took a step and was immediately on the other side of it.

I suggested she turn around and step back into it one more time. She did and instantly was on the other side of the wormhole. She was back in the room with the triangular doors. This time she could see other places. She could go other ways.

Sacred Geometries

Stephanie asked Wisdom to choose where she should go next. Having asked Wisdom to choose where she should go next, she took three steps and was surrounded by equations and mechanical engineering. It had an engineering feel to her. It was as if she was in outer space and seeing all of this, but it was in a bubble. Some books were suspended, and there were geometric equations all around.

She was drawn to one of the books, so she touched it. It was suspended in the air, and she could open it and flip the pages. It was written in Hebrew. Although she could not read Hebrew, she took the pair of glasses lying on top of the book, looked up the word "focus," and read, "something that has multiple interests or activities; to pay particular attention to."

She chose to pay particular attention to the book, 'Geometries.' It was a book of sacred geometries. She did not feel like she was supposed to read it but just knew it was about sacred geometry, not just geometry.

She then saw another thing suspended in the air. It was like an oil decanter. She picked it up to look closer at the bottle. It reminded her of the one that the scarecrow had to use for the tin man in the Wizard of Oz movie. It was the substance of illumination. It was a new tool for her toolbelt that she could use when walking in these paradigms. She asked Wisdom to do whatever needed to be done with the substance of illumination.

She prayed:

I ask for the substance of illumination everywhere we go. I ask for the sacred geometries to be opened to us in Jesus' name.

Now it was as if the entire thing that looked like outer space was now in color. There were brilliant colors everywhere—pink colors, blues, and greens that she had never seen before. It was a picture of what was coming. She added this to her tool belt.

We were then back in the Exchange Room. Stephanie prayed,

I request and take all the knowledge I've received and ask for help to piece this together from this experience. I don't understand it all, but I'm laying it on the exchange table to be returned to me— knowledge, wisdom, and understanding.

We were informed that the passes on the lanyards that we had received earlier were ours to keep. We could come into the exchange room anytime we wanted.

———·———

Chapter 16
The Kingdom Dynamic
of the Peace Bond

This engagement with Heaven involved information for our Senior Advocates but will be helpful to every son. We saw what looked like soul ties to the original formats of how the Personal Advocacy Sessions were conducted. *Soul tie* is not the right word, but that is what it looked like—a tether to LifeSpring's earlier format of how things were done with the Outstanding Folder, etc.

We saw not a cutting or severing of those ties but a stretching. Those that work on behalf of clients can become comfortable with this stretching. They have been walking in a norm, and this new work is getting outside of it. It's making them uncomfortable, which is what their soul is feeling, which is why it feels like conflict. The enemy is trying to bring confusion concerning this.

Ezekiel reminded us that the prophets of old were never walking in comfort. They experienced continual stretching, constant bending and turning to the Lord's ways, His ears, and His steps. It was a true stretch. This stretching can feel uncomfortable. It can seem unnatural. Being comfortable creates stagnation. What we do is not comfortable work. We do not provide a comfortable product. We are not going to stay in any pattern. There will be constant growth.

---

*With constant growth,
there will be growing pains.*

Our intercessors must continually release Bonds of Ease upon the Juniors, Seniors, and Student Observers, as well as Bonds of Trust. It's serious work."

Father, we commend Ezekiel, his commanders, and ranks to you.

We ask on their behalf angel food, bread and elixir, every armament of Heaven that is available and needed, and every capturing bag of every color, size, and dimension.

Ezekiel, we commission you, your commanders, and ranks to work on behalf of the ministry, for every person that works for the ministry, to capture every infiltration, witchcraft, and any and everything else in every age, realm, dimension, and timeline, in time and out of time.

We commission you to work with the angels of the Seniors, Juniors, and Observers to partner with their angels and to bring these bonds upon them in the name of Jesus.

Father, we ask to step into the Court of Titles and Deeds. On behalf of LifeSpring International, its team members, Juniors, Seniors, and those that are observing, we request a Bond of Ease and a Bond of Trust regarding the trusts.

We ask that it be placed upon their records and their realms and that it be released on their behalf and ours for the sake of the Kingdom for, 'Thy Kingdom come, and thy will be done on earth as it is in Heaven.'

Father, we ask for a release of the Peace Bond upon their books and records and upon ours in Jesus' name.

We immediately received the righteous verdict of the release of a Peace Bond for each of them so the enemy could not continue his work of confusion.

Chapter 17

The Kingdom Dynamic of the Spirit of Understanding

As we engaged Heaven, Enoch joined us and was eating a plum. He exclaimed, "I'm all about the verse in the Word, 'Taste and see the Lord is good,' so I'm tasting." In several engagements with Enoch, he has always been resting and usually enjoying pie or dessert. We asked, "What do you want to help us know?"

Enoch replied, "I don't want to help you *know*; I'm GOING to help you taste! Why wouldn't you want to use ALL of the senses in Heaven? Your sense of taste on earth is pale compared to the senses alive in Heaven."

In the spirit, the verse 2 Chronicles 2:13 was heard.

And now I have sent a skillful man, <u>endowed with understanding</u>, Huram, my master craftsman.

We reread it seeking to grasp what Enoch wanted us to know.

"I've sent a skillful man endowed with understanding."

Enoch impressed upon us that not only was Huram a skillful man endowed with understanding, but so is Enoch, and so are we in the Father's eyes.

This engagement was about the Spirit of Understanding. Enoch inquired, "Do you understand what you're tasting when you eat it?"

We replied that we did, and then he showed us a blindfold challenge; when someone is blindfolded and tastes something, they know exactly what it is. They understand what it is in that moment.

We were getting to the simplicity of the matter. We have all been tasting a portion of Heaven in our engagements.

Enoch said, "If you can do a blindfold challenge and know what you're eating, then when you step into Heaven, and you sense, see, or know, how is it that so many still don't know? Have them taste the goodness of God."

Stephanie asked, "Would you say they already have because they are stepping in?"

Enoch replied, "I would say, if they've already tasted the goodness of God by the access into Heaven, why don't they savor it?"

"Taste and see. These are open-door opportunities to engage with the King of kings and Lord of lords. Tell me, when have men known this availability before?"

We replied, "You knew it, Enoch."

Enoch explained, "That's right, because I was one of the ones that was a skillful man endowed with understanding. It is because I sought knowledge, the Kingdom, and understanding, and that's how YOU can *now* taste and see. That is how I could taste and see, and ultimately never die.

"Many people seek the fountain of youth because they don't want to die. Why don't they seek this instead?"

Stephanie answered, "Well, Enoch, is it because the church failed?"

He reminded her of our engagement a few days prior about making what we get out of Heaven an idol. When we seek Heaven for the end game—for what we could get out of Heaven instead of seeking relationship with the Father, we have made the end result an idol instead of developing relationship with the Father. He leaned in, and said, "tell them to taste and see."

"With this, people will have their vision of being able to see like they want to see or experience Heaven the way they want.

"Experiencing Heaven comes by seeking Understanding (the entity). It is one of the Seven Spirits of God!"[10]

Enoch began eating a pie, and we asked what kind.

Enoch replied, "Rhubarb pie. It's my favorite."

To taste and see, we must seek the Kingdom through Understanding—one of the Seven Spirits of God.

We welcomed Understanding, and as soon as we did, the entity Understanding walked in. We had met Knowledge before, but when Understanding came, he had oil with him.

Understanding lights the way—He provides illumination. Wisdom illuminates in one and Understanding illuminates in another way.

David began reading from The Mirror Bible,

I desire that you would draw directly from the source that the God of our Lord Jesus' Christ to Father in glory, kindles within you, the spirit of wisdom and revelation in the unveiling of his master plan, I long for you to know by revelation, what he has known about you all along, his intent is doxa glory. Paul suggests that we might find our source in God's knowledge, in what it is that he knows about us to know. Even as we have always been known, dealing with wisdom and

---

[10] Isaiah 11:2

understanding and revelation the eyes of our understanding would be enlightened. (Ephesians 1:17) (MIRROR)

Your word is a lamp to my feet and a light to my path. (Psalms 119:105)

The entity Understanding is also known as the Lamp of Understanding, which is why Understanding presented himself as oil, because lamps were usually lit with oil in ancient times. We asked Understanding to pour his oil upon us.

Our heart's desire is that the Lamp of Understanding work with us, LifeSpring, all the entities of LifeSpring, all those that draw near to it, and their families. We asked how to do that and were told to draw it out.

Truth's shining light guides me in my choices and decisions; the revelation of your word makes my pathway clear. (Psalm 119:105) (TPT)

We asked Understanding how we draw this out. How do we receive this?

We were told that it requires seeking. Seeking the Kingdom draws the light of Understanding. It also provides the flavor to taste because oil has a flavor.

We remarked to Understanding that we wanted to draw from him and that we had been seeking the Kingdom. As soon as we said that, he started pouring the oil upon us.

Understanding added, "Seek first the Kingdom of God and all of these things will be added unto you. The light of His Glory shines upon you. Truth. Understanding Complexities. Revelation. Heart. Belonging. Son. Love. Tell your spirits to rise up! Tell the Glory—stand up!"

Begin to call your spirit forward and tell it to rise up. Then tell the Glory to stand up. This is how this is received. Do it! Glory, Stand up. Our spirit receives the Light of the Understanding—the lamp, the oil.

Stephanie asked, "Understanding, you said, 'taste and see.' Will you give it to Adina and let her see something right now?"

Understanding said, "Adina, my beloved, what do you see?"

Adina explained, "I see banquet tables set with all kinds of food, fruits, and vegetables. Delicious looking foods."

Understanding said, "Taste."

Stephanie said, "Adina, these are the eyes of your understanding. It's not your natural eyes. It is your spirit man's eyes. It will tell your soul; your soul will see, and your body will see. These are the eyes of your understanding.

"It's as if I saw two eyeballs being handed to you. Why not? Because they are the eyes of your understanding! Look at what you saw!"

Adina replied, "And it was immediate. I just closed my eyes here, so I wasn't distracted."

Stephanie said, "Thank you for the oil and the Lamp of Understanding. Thank you for the words from Heaven that come with this oil and Understanding. Understanding, you are quite amazingly intricate and beautiful."

The whole time this had been happening, Enoch stood here, but he had been very quiet.

Understanding asked Stephanie, "What measure do you require?"

She replied, "I want unlimited!"

Understanding asked David the same question. He replied, "I want as much as you can pour out upon me. I want all the Understanding of what Heaven has, what Heaven is, and what God is. I want an abundance of Understanding, the revelation. I can go on and on and on."

Spirit of Understanding said, "What measure I bring is what measure you give."

Stephanie inquired, "Understanding, you're saying that what you are bringing and giving to us—the measure you bring to us, we are going to be able to bring Understanding to others because of the measure that we have?"

"Yes," Spirit of Understanding replied.

Enoch interjected, "Isn't that just like the Father? It's not just giving it to us, or for us; it's giving it to us for others."

Stephanie replied, "Understanding, we ask for the measure from you that is ours, that the Father has for us, for ourselves, the measure of Understanding to others."

Spirit of Understanding remarked, "I am the light unto the path."

We paused to thank the Father for all we had been experiencing. While we were doing so, Understanding repositioned himself and was positioned above the entity that looks like and reminds me of a star, the entity of LifeSpring, and other stars around it, which are all the people. He was above it all. He began pouring out measures of Understanding onto the entity that is LifeSpring. It was a positioning. He positioned himself and was no longer moving. This was a new positioning that we had not seen before.

David commented, "I wrote this down some time ago, and I heard this. Enoch had asked me a question, 'What happens when you chew on something?'"

Adina replied, "You break it down so you can swallow it and digest it."

David responded, "Then Enoch said, 'Chew, chew, chew on it! And get Understanding.' Then I heard, 'With all your getting, get understanding.'"[11]

"This is what I have been experiencing while you were talking. That's why I was quiet because, at some point, I began to see a book before me, like a journal. But I couldn't see the words, yet the words were coming, and I was writing, writing, and reading. It was my scroll. As I was sitting, receiving, it was going to my spirit. My spirit man already knew; he knows what's in the book. Because I began to read and flip through the pages and read, but my conscience, my soul, is on a different level. My spirit man was receiving or getting the deposit or a download."

Stephanie asked, "Our spirit man must chew on it; do we instruct our souls to digest this?"

David replied, "Yes."

Stephanie added, "Well, I'm going to say, as an act of faith, I'm going to reach out, and I'm going to get understanding by the arm, and I'm going to bring you into myself." Each of us did similarly.

> *[1] My son, if you receive my words, And treasure my commands within you, [2] so that you incline your ear to wisdom, And apply your heart to understanding; [3] yes, if you cry out for discernment, And lift up your voice for understanding, [4] if you seek her as silver, And*

---

[11] Proverbs 4:7

search for her as for hidden treasures; ⁵ then you will understand the fear of the LORD, And find the knowledge of God.

⁶ For the LORD gives wisdom; From His mouth come knowledge and understanding; ⁷ He stores up sound wisdom for the upright; He is a shield to those who walk uprightly; ⁸ He guards the paths of justice, And preserves the way of His saints. (Proverbs 2:1-8)

Stephanie continued, "For me, in my process, I've been introduced to and had conversations with and have held hands with Wisdom. I have seen Knowledge one time and he shook my hand, but I have just taken hold of Understanding.

"I've been asking the Father, I want to experience the reverential fear of the Lord because I don't know what that means. I know what it means here (in my head), but I don't know what it means here (in my heart); not that I am afraid of the Lord, in some ways in a healthy fear. Yes, I know there's a reverential fear of the Lord. I have yet to experience it. What you just read was we get Wisdom, then we gain Knowledge, then we gain Understanding, then we get the reverential Fear of the Lord. Is that what it looks like in that verse? Is that the path?

"It's Wisdom, Knowledge, Understanding, and then the referential Fear of the Lord."

Ron noted, "Verse 5 says, 'and you'll understand the Fear of the Lord and find the Knowledge of God.' Otherwise, you won't respect the knowledge."

Stephanie added, "We're in Phase Two; we've met Wisdom, and now we have met Understanding."

David said, "This is the Geneva Bible:

If you will receive my words and hide my commandments within thee, and cause thine ears to hearken to my wisdom, your heart to understanding, or if I call after knowledge and cry after understanding, if you seek her as wisdom and seek her as for treasure, then you shall understand the fear of the Lord and find the knowledge God. For such that he preserves the state of the righteous. He is a shield to them that walk uprightly.

Wisdom is a gift from a generous God, and every word he speaks is full of revelation and becomes a fountain of understanding within you. (Proverbs 2:6) (TPT)

So train your heart to listen when I speak and open your spirit wide to expand your discernment—then pass it on to your sons and daughters. ³ Yes, cry out for comprehension and intercede for insight. ⁴ For if you keep seeking it like a man would seek for sterling silver, searching in hidden places for cherished treasure, ⁵ then you will discover the fear of the Lord and find the true knowledge of God. (Proverbs 2:2-5) (TPT)

Now we could see Enoch, and we still saw Understanding. Enoch went back to eating and he was grinning from ear to ear.

Enoch said, "It was my good pleasure to be a part of this engagement."

Stephanie noted, "He showed me this was part of his redemption. Not everybody gets to walk with the Seven Spirits of God in Heaven except those that have earned it or are still earning it."

David commented, "We need that oil to illuminate so we can understand what the Word is saying, what our Father is saying so we can take it in. That's how we take it in, then apply it and let it change us."

———·———

Chapter 18
The Kingdom Dynamic of the Entity of Prudence

We asked to step into the Courts of Heaven regarding our biweekly check-ins for LifeSpring International Ministries. Gloria was there to meet us, a woman in white who serves as our legal counsel in the Courts. She had an accordion file with her and said there was a docket number: 1457.

It had been filed on our behalf regarding interrogation measures by the enemy. It was because the enemy came against the Lord's work.

Stephanie asked, "May I ask the importance of that docket number 1, 4, 5, 7?"

Our Council said, "Numbers are important to the Lord."

[Pondering this later, I chose to look up Strong's Concordance definition for the Hebrew and the Greek words under 1457. The Hebrew word is *gahar* which means to prostrate oneself. It is found 3 times in the Old Testament. Once, Elijah went to the top of Mount Carmel and fell down upon his face before the Lord. The other two instances were when Elisha laid upon the young boy who had died and revived him.

In the New Testament, the Greek word (G1457) *egkainizo* means consecrating or dedicating oneself. It was used in the New Testament in two instances. One refers to a sacrificial animal, and the other speaks of Jesus, who laid down his life for us. He consecrated Himself on our behalf.

We asked if there were any cases we needed to file in the Courts of Heaven. The impression was to request a case be filed against covetousness for anyone that has drawn near to the ministry or is a part of the ministry, and to file it in court. We also requested annihilation of that covetousness, angelic assistance, and we requested the verdict of the Father. Stephanie could see the Father calling in someone and talking to them in the courtroom.

Father, whoever it is, we would like to state that we forgive that person.

We repent on their behalf because we know a spirit is using them.

We ask for the blood to cover their sin, bless them, and we release them in Jesus' name.

Ezekiel and the Beast

Stephanie requested Ezekiel to draw near. She could see that he was quite far from her but could tell he was holding a huge lasso. He had lassoed a mighty beast. He was not having any trouble, but he was very small compared to this beast. Ezekiel had all the assistance he needed.

Answering on Ezekiel's behalf, we were told, concerning the beast, that the mightier the beast, the harder they fall.

The commander was also holding some strategies and maps in his hand, so Stephanie made a request to the Father.

Father, we request the strategies, maps, and keys for Ezekiel, his commanders, and ranks, and we thank you, Father, for the lasso you have given him to bring down the mighty beast. The mightier they are, the harder they fall. We thank you for their fall.

We request angel food, bread, and elixir of all the flavors for every angel—the flavor they love and the key, the new armaments in the warehouse, the new warehouse, and every armament is available.

We commission you to use the shields, the veils, the smoke bombs against the enemy, and every capture bag of every color, size, and dimension in the name of Jesus.

We commission you to fully use those strategies, those maps, and those keys on behalf of LifeSpring and everyone that draws near to it in Jesus's name.

Taxes & Reclamation

George appeared to discuss the subject of taxes. He pointed out that the enemy had taxed us. It came in the form of an attack. We were told we could go to the Court of Reclamations and present filings outlining the taxing that was done. George had kept a record of everything that had taxed the ministry. It was part of his duties. He accompanied us to court per our request as we went to the Court of Reclamations.

We ask to step into the Court of Reclamations on behalf of LifeSpring International Ministries, and we have George here with us.

We gave counsel for the file of the taxations to be taken to the Just Judge.

Just Judge, we present this record of taxations against LifeSpring and request knowledge and counsel on what can be reclaimed.

The Judge responded that we were being given acceleration and assigned the entity of Prudence.

I welcomed Prudence on behalf of the ministry. At the same time, the Judge gave George keys to access the King's Treasury because what was stolen and taxed was taken directly from the Kingdom. The King has a storehouse where the angels have been plundering the enemies' camp, bringing things back to the storehouses. He gave George access to the King's Treasury to recover what was stolen financially. The Judge also commended George for his diligence.

We also were given what was called "protective arms." It had a double meaning, as in arms, as in weaponry, but also arms, as in the protection of the Father's arms.

We have already seen the first stages of the reclamation of expanse (a directive we were given from Heaven that you can read more about in chapter 26), but more is coming. With acceleration, we must become expansive. It is the heart of the Father for ministries to grow and accomplish all that is in their scroll and govern every territory the Father desires for us. Our enemy resists that expansion and to deal with the resistance requires boldness and courage. LifeSpring had experienced this sort of resistance, but Heaven wanted it restored to us. In the process, the judge informed us that we would be given the White Glove Treatment.

The definition of the White Glove Treatment is to provide a very high level of service which involves a lot of care about the small details.

We asked George if anything was needed relating to the additional office space we had acquired. George said that he would get what he needed from the King's Treasury.

We were acquiring some additional office space and asked Lydia if we needed to do anything in preparation for it. We were told to obtain the Amendment of Justification of All Things, where this additional space is added into the White Glove Treatment with very detailed information.

This amendment is Heaven down[12], but it's as if we are moving into that place, and this amendment opens the gates for many more new things. It is like there is a portal with French doors at the back of the business. It opens directly into Heaven and even though I know it is in the spirit, it feels so close like it is in the natural. It is a part of our expanse, the amendment of expanse.[13] It was directly from the Court of Reclamation and part of the expanse was included in this amendment.

We were informed that we would be there only a short time, and that the ministry would expand fast!

———·———

[12] To conduct business or ministry from Heaven down, is to consult with Heaven first for instruction, not merely come up with an idea and ask God to bless it.

[13] Discussed more in Chapter 26.

Chapter 19

The Kingdom Dynamic of Grace Abounding

As Stephanie and I stepped into Heaven to engage this day; we saw the ocean and were sitting on a beach. Jesus was sitting beside Stephanie, and he began to sing in the spirit. As he sang, a very silvery looking being began to arise from the water, not unlike the creature in the Terminator movies. Asking who we were seeing, we were told it was the entity—Grace.

We were told that Grace would be walking with us. Grace sat down on the other side of Jesus, as he continued to sing. Then, the scene shifted somewhat, and Peter appeared. Stephanie had been given a stack of files and she asked Peter what these files were that she was to talk to him about.

Peter began to explain,

Grace is an entity.

It took Peter a while to walk with Grace when he was walking upon the earth. Jesus revealed many things that were entities to the disciples, but we didn't have much understanding about them until after Jesus returned to Heaven. At this point the disciples began to have their own encounters, walking through the realms of Heaven and learning these things. They then met this entity—Grace Abounding[14], who also walked with them. Jesus equipped them with more than what they could imagine, more than what is written.

Scripture says,

> *Where sin abounds, grace abounds much more (Roman 6:1).*

Peter was not walking with Grace when he denied Jesus. We understood from him that we could call upon Grace as an entity to walk with us as we do with Wisdom.

The Scripture says that we are to *seek after wisdom*, but *grace abounds*, the two different entities are found two different ways in your walk with the Father.

---

*Grace can be given out and
Grace can abound from you to others.*

---

[14] Grace and Grace Abounding are the same entity.

Remember the Scriptures, where Paul would say, "Peace to you," and "Grace to you." They were giving a portion *of their portion of Grace to others*, but...

The entity Grace always fills the giver back up.

In the spirit, the New Testament saints took what looked like a measuring spoon and when they would say "Grace to you," they took a piece of the entity Grace, and gave it to the recipient and she abounded in that moment in their lives.

Grace never diminishes when you release Grace to another.

How do we apply this?

Just as we speak Peace to someone, speak Grace. You can give fuller measures. You may realize someone needs a fuller measure of the entity of Grace than someone else. In the moment of praying with or ministering to someone, speak Peace and ask that it rest upon them—Peace and Grace are given.

We wanted the entity Grace to abound with everyone in LifeSpring and their families, and we found that we could request that Grace may abound much in each of those in the LifeSpring family.

Father, I would like to put in a request, please.

I would like to request Jesus that you would have Grace as an entity abound upon everyone that is associated with and draws near to LifeSpring and their families and upon the entity of LifeSpring itself, CoursNet, Heaven Down Business, the books, AfterCare, LifeSpring Publishing, and Sandhills Ecclesia.[15]

I Corinthians 15:58,

Therefore, my beloved brethren be ye steadfast unmovable, always abounding in the work of the Lord for as much as you know that your labor is not in vain.

Abound means to exist in large numbers or amounts.

We can also use Abounding Grace as a godly bond.

Having made the request for Grace to abound, the files that were in her hand came forth. They were Certificates of Grace Abounding. The first one was for Stephanie, and the other files were for all those she had made a request on behalf of. At the same time, Grace in Stephanie was not diminished.

Stephanie continued,

---

[15] These are not all the entities of LifeSpring but major ones.

I request from the Court of Titles & Deeds, the godly bond of Abounding Grace, in Jesus' name for all of those that draw near to LifeSpring Ministries and the entities of LifeSpring International Ministries and all their families in Jesus' name. I ask that these be recorded today and placed on everyone's registry.

I ask the Bond Registry Angels to work with all the angels of those whom I have requested bonds for and bring them to their realms in Jesus' name.

Romans 5:20-21:

The presence of the law made no difference. Instead, it merely highlighted the offense, but where sin increased Grace superseded it. ^{21}Death provided sin its platform and power to reign from now. Grace has taken over sovereignty through righteousness to introduce unthreatened life under the Lordship of Jesus Christ over us. (MIRROR)

———·———

Chapter 20
The Kingdom Dynamic
of Digging Deeper

The visual was of an operating theater with the focus on the light that hung above the table. It was extremely bright. It illuminated places like no other light source could do. It enabled the surgeon to probe and operate with great precision. This light lit up even the smallest areas of darkness. Essentially, no darkness can hide in this kind of light.

Would you trust this illumination on its own to guarantee perfect surgery, or is anything else needed?

The only thing else needed is to trust the physician's hand—trusting and knowing that He knows where and how deep to go to expose the darkness. The light is not the physician—the light is the revelation.

Heaven has released a lot of revelation recently, and more is coming. The additional understanding is realizing revelation brings the light and illumination, uncovering the darkness (including the dark things in us). People are missing *the trust factor* of trusting the surgeon's hand. The Great Physician is moving things out of the way to get right into the depth of the matter. This is the heart of the matter.

The question that people need to ask themselves is why they trust the revelation and not the Great Physician's hand?

How deep are you willing to let the surgeon go to get to the heart of the matter?

Do we trust the 'digging in deep,' the revealing, and the exposure of the darkness to light?

We must-each of us.

How deep are we willing to go? This is a question for people to ask themselves, **'How deep are we willing to go, and how deep are we willing to let the Father go?'"**

The Fortress

The next vision was of a fortress which was deeply fortified, and we could see Ezekiel. We asked him to tell us about this fortress that looked as if it was being defended. We were told to look deeper.

It was like one of those fortresses you would see in medieval times. The drawbridge was up. It had a moat around it and guards at the top with arrows, ready to strike.

Ezekiel showed us there were places of weakness in the fortress. There were weaknesses around this fortified place that the enemy absolutely could get in.

We asked if this image was about LifeSpring or individuals who had well-fortified territories with weaknesses around them. We wanted to know how to shore the weak places up.

> *Ezekiel, I commission you to come in where a foundational issue or movement needs to be fortified.*

We kept hearing the word *dunamis*. Ezekiel said that we needed to fortify this to cause it to be solid. We saw just one place that needed fortifying, but it was a foundational cornerstone area.

> *I request the release of dunamis power to fill in every gap and every weak point in that foundation.*

The fortifying happened immediately. It became hard as steel.

Again, we were asked how deep we were willing to go. Our reply was to go pretty deep.

We need to ask ourselves. "**How deep are we willing to let the Great Physician go who doesn't just heal physical ailments, but emotional, mental, spiritual,**

and physical ailments as well? He is the one who came and bore our sicknesses and our diseases. The one that every stripe that was laid upon his back opened the way for the illumination and the light to expose every darkness of our life. Each person needs to ask themselves, "How deep are we willing to go with this?"

It is not just about revelation. Revelation is the light, but it's *the cooperation with the Great Physician,* the cooperation with the one who can move things around to expose where darkness is hidden in the heart. Are they willing to do that?

Are we willing to go there in our own lives? And if so, when we say "Yes," more illumination and freedom will emerge in our lives.

Are we willing to fortify our foundations? Are we willing to ask the questions that need to be asked of the Father with the help of their angels to expose the places that the enemy could get into? Some must deal with the heart of the matter.

Many, including myself, have been very excited about all the new revelation, but with revelation comes illumination of the dark regions in our lives that we must allow to be exposed. What does a physician do when he moves those things out of the way and digs deeper to find dark places, the roots of disease, to bring forth the healing? This is healing.

I say to Heaven, take those places in my heart, illuminate them, and dig deeper for healing.

I request on behalf of those who work for, contract with, volunteer for, and draw near to the ministry that the Great Physician begin to go into those places we have fortified well because of the revelation of the Courts of Heaven. We have strategically put fortifications around doing all this generational work, but there are weaknesses around some of the foundations.

Father, illuminate each of our hearts as this revelation comes.

I commission the angels assigned to me to go in with dunamis power in my own life and the lives of those around us—those that draw near to us, and fortify—like steel, with the dunamis power around the foundations and deep trenches of our lives and in our hearts, to do this around and in the cornerstones of who we are with the dunamis power, with the blood of Jesus, and in the name of Jesus.

Ezekiel, I commission you to put your commanders and ranks strategically around the places that need fortifying and to continue to make sure the foundation is solid around the entities that are LifeSpring, Sandhills Ecclesia, CourtsNet, Adina's Melodies, and Heaven Down Business, and all the other aspects of LifeSpring.

I ask for the blood of Jesus and living water to be the wellspring of life over all these entities and over all of those that draw near, in Jesus' name.

Father, we commend the angels to you.

I ask for angel food, bread, and elixir.

I request the armaments of Heaven, Truth Defender Membrane, and we request the awakening angels.

I ask for the illumination in Jesus' name.

It was such an interesting manner in which Heaven took us down that path. The people around us are excited about the new revelation and they are drinking it in, but some have been, or all of us maybe, have been piling that revelation on top of places where there still needed to be some exposure of darkness and where, deep in our lives, things need to be uncovered as the Lord peels all these things back in our lives. It's a clarion call for the body to know that there is something we still need to allow the Lord to do to accomplish this deep, deep work in our lives.

———·———

Chapter 21
The Kingdom Dynamic of Illumination

In the Court of Records, we heard the phrase "Blinded by the Light." Curious to understand the meaning. I sensed that some of the people who view our meetings or read our materials were overwhelmed by the amount of revelation.

Wanting direction as to what to do or where to go in the Courts of Heaven for these people who are blinded by the light, we determined that we were dealing with a false verdict that said the light would blind the people.

We began:

Your honor, we ask to step into your Appellate Court, please. We have been made aware that there is a false verdict against the ministry and against the teachings of this ministry, against the revelation that's coming from Heaven to this ministry. We are requesting an overturning of this false verdict from hell.

Father, you are the revelation. This is all about You and Your Kingdom.

We ask for the blood of Jesus to satisfy this and Father, anyone that has accused us or has felt in any way regarding this.

We ask to bring them in where they have had these thoughts and even come into agreement that 'this is too much revelation'—blinded by the light.

Your honor, we repent on their behalf for believing the lie—and that's what it is. It is a lie.

We repent on their behalf and ask for the blood of Jesus to cover it. We forgive, bless, and release them and ask to step into the Court of Decrees, Your Honor.

The decree to be made had to come from my mouth as the leader of LifeSpring, so I began.

I decree that there will be illumination by the revelation as opposed to blindness by the revelation that is released from Heaven to LifeSpring International Ministries, and there should be an embrace of the revelation by hungry hearts all over the globe in Jesus' name.

Stephanie then saw the gavel come down.

We were then instructed to step into the Court of Titles and Deeds and request a bond for all those who draw near to the ministry, those who are coming to the ministry, and those who have perhaps fallen away from the ministry because they felt blinded by the light. Having accessed the Court of Titles and Deeds, we began:

We request a Bond of Excellence, a Bond of Illumination, and a Bond of Revelatory Knowledge and Understanding.

We ask that these be released upon their realms, upon their records, upon the entity of LifeSpring International ministries, and their families in the name of Jesus.

We must recognize that it is a plot of the enemy for us to become dismayed by what our soul perceives as a revelation overload. Our soul may want to assert a position of being a gatekeeper for revelation when that is not its department. Your spirit is the realm that receives revelation from Heaven and dispenses it as needed to your soul and body. When your soul is weary, help shore it up by praying in tongues. Your soul may even resist you doing so. Sometimes you need to pray strongly in tongues and cause the well within you to bubble up.

You will also need to instruct your soul to rest. It is not the job of your soul to figure out revelation. That job belongs to your spirit. Your spirit will dispense the revelation to your soul in terms that your soul can comprehend. This is likely to happen after the receipt of new revelation. It usually takes time.

You will also need to ensure that you are spirit-forward. The sense of overload will not likely occur when you are spirit-forward. When in a setting where new revelation will be released, we must be sure to position our spirit in the forward position. It is difficult to receive revelation when your spirit is in park. It needs **to be forward and moving.**

Also, if we find our soul is wanting everything to be verified by a load of Scriptures, that is a throwback to the Tree of the Knowledge of Good and Evil wanting to reassert dominance in your thinking. Revelation will be confirmed by Scripture, but the Father is not trying to validate our theology.

The spirit of religion despises revelation because it cannot control it.

Because of that, you may need to do court work regarding the soul and its attachment to the Tree of the Knowledge of Good and Evil and the spirit of religion wanting to arise. You may need to make a fresh surrender to the Father, deeding the territory of your mind and thought processes to the Lord. You also may need to divorce yourself from the Tree of the Knowledge of Good and Evil. It opposes the working of the Tree of Life.

> *We must guard against
> the accusation of revelation overload.*

It will kill the flow of Heaven into your life that your spirit has longed for so deeply. It will open doors of strife and dissension against those who are the instruments delivering the revelation. They are simply seeking to follow the instruction of Heaven in dispensing the revelation received.

Those delivering the revelation are dealing with similar challenges from the enemy as he wants to shut down the flow of revelation to the Body of Christ. Let us not give our enemy the satisfaction of having done so.

Chapter 22
The Kingdom Dynamic of Thirst

This engagement included some new experiences for Stephanie. She described that she found herself standing in front of a short palm tree that was about her height.

The palm tree spoke and asked a question, "Does this give you shade?"

"No," Stephanie replied. She then looked to her left and saw a taller palm tree which was about the typical height for a palm tree.

It asked, "Does this give you shade?"

Stephanie responded, "No, it doesn't give me shade either." Continuing, she said, "By the way, I now realize I am in a desert. It is very bright, and you can tell that there is very little shade around. I see an oasis with water, and multiple palm trees around. I can see that when they are clustered together, there is shade. She walked to the cluster of trees and felt compelled to lean over and take water in her hand and drink it.

Immediately, a camel appeared beside her, and they were both drinking simultaneously. Stephanie was startled when she realized the camel was next to her. She remarked, "We have startled each other. We are both looking at each other."

Then she greeted the camel and heard it say, "Hello, Stephanie. Does a camel need shade?"

Stephanie replied, "You know, I don't think so." The camel began showing her the humps on its back. It has reservoirs of water stored inside of it.

The camel then sat down beside her.

The camel explained, "No. We do not need shade. However, there is a point in time that we must fill ourselves. Although, on the journey, the living water is stored inside of us."

Stephanie explained, "I am seeing a picture of this camel in the desert, and it feels like he has been walking for hours and hours, but he has not been overcome by the heat or by being out in the exposed elements because of the reservoir of water inside of him.

"Now, I can see that we're back at the Oasis."

The camel asked, "How much more could the sons be in the "elements," and under the 'scorching' of everyday life if only they understood they have the reservoir of living water inside of them, all the time."

> *You have a reservoir of living water
> inside you all the time.*

Stephanie replied, "I would say that we would be able to walk in a much higher place knowing that and understanding that specific principle."

The camel asked, "How did we first meet? "

Stephanie answered, "We first met while you were also drinking from this oasis."

The camel replied, "The principal is still there that we must fill ourselves to have a substantial amount of living water, to walk in life in the elements."

Stephanie explained, "As soon as he said, elements, the spiritual realm opened, and I can see the demonic, the attacks, the things that would be coming against the sons, and I can see being able to stand as a son with zero fear with the understanding that the living water of Heaven is a reservoir that we can be filled from. I see the spiritual realm coming against this camel, but it is unaffected. It just keeps walking. It just keeps walking as if nothing is happening around it."

Stephanie said to the camel, "The sense that I'm getting from you, camel, is that it is time with the Father—that precious intimacy with the Father—where we are refilled."

The camel replied, "Yes, it is so refreshing."

Stephanie continued, "Camel. I feel like the story for today is around knowing the simple picture of the reservoir that is within us. When we drink from the fountain, the living water, the elements cannot touch us. The strength that you walked in, not even bothered by the time that you were out in the elements and in the scorching heat. You were not bothered by the spiritual realm coming against you. This is a straightforward picture, yet it is profound. Thank you, camel."

The camel paused, took an enormous drink of water out of the oasis, stood up and moved back onto his journey saying, "I bless you all in your journey."

———·———

Chapter 23
The Kingdom Dynamic of Wisdom Constructs

We had been engaging with our counsel and our special guest that day—Jesus. He had just exited the Conference Room when Wisdom said, "Wisdom Constructs."

Stephanie replied, "Okay. We're back to this. Constructive Trusts!"

Wisdom said, "Even the hole in which the cross was placed that was dug for that day was a construct, a foundation of what was coming. Our Savior's death, burial, and resurrection was part of the foundation that has led us to this day. In this day, His sons and His daughters have full access to the Seven Spirits of God, Jesus, and to the Ancient of Days anytime they want.

"Every word that was spoken out of Jesus's mouth was a foundation, a Constructive Trust laid out and building the bridge that closed the gap. With these

Constructive Trusts that you are teaching, you are building bridges in people's lives out of this work. These are powerful tools. You'll be learning more about Constructive Trusts as they are a dominion themselves—a godly dominion taking the place over the order of the old dominion the sons are laying waste as they do this work. This is for such a time as this. This is bringing the Glory upon the earth. The earth has cried out for this. This generation—THIS generation is bringing it to pass.

Stephanie, weeping, said, "Hallelujah! Hallelujah, Father. Halleluiah that You deemed us worthy."

She continued, "He is showing me that those who call their innocence back, will understand their time with the Father before He created the earth when they stood before Him as Innocents. His sons are beginning to see, understand, know, and feel the time where they were with him before the foundations of the earth. If you could hear the joyous cries—not crying but the shouts.

Wisdom reiterated, "This is taking shape upon the earth." This is rolling and billowing forth. The stride is strong, and each step perfectly syncs with Jesus."

Stephanie said, "Wisdom just reminded me of that day when we could look down at our feet and see Jesus walking in step with us. There's that Scripture again, "No greater love hath a man than one who lays down his life for a friend." She's showing me that this is exactly what the Scripture means about loving your neighbor. That's what we are doing through this ministry. We're interacting with perfect strangers and laying down pieces of our life on behalf of them and their generations which is why the glory is here. It's coming! It's now! What I just saw was threefold: It's here, it's coming, and it's now."

Stephanie to Wisdom, "Thank you, Wisdom; I'm so glad you are here."

Alicia then sat down, putting a binder on the table, saying aloud, "Great growth is coming. This is what trading is."

Stephanie said to Alicia, "I understand, Alicia what Heaven showed us yesterday about trading, how everything that we do as a good trade, Jesus and the Father multiply it, and that's what this is, isn't it?"

She replied, "These are the rules of multiplication."

Malcolm sat at the table, and Stephanie could sense he had much to speak about. Stephanie described what she saw: "He has a lot of what look like plans that an architect would have. There is page after page after page. These blueprints represent what is coming; this is what we will be learning."

Lydia had just presented herself when she said to Stephanie, "This is going to take your full agreement."

Stephanie responded, "I fully agree. I know Ron fully agrees. You know I don't like testing."

Lydia said, "But a testing will come out of this."

Stephanie remarked, "It's not the kind of testing where Jesus is just wanting to see if we're going to pass, it's not that. I fully accept whatever it is because I trust Heaven."

Stephanie described what she saw. When I said that I trust Heaven, Lydia turned and handed the paperwork to Ezekiel, who (I realize now) was standing there wearing his breastplate and crown. She handed the paperwork to him, and he smiled at Ron shaking his head up and down. He then smiled at me. He then took the paperwork and left. I just saw, as he turned, that he was holding a lot of individual pieces of paper, and on each one was a small arrow attached to the top and Ezekiel said, "It will pierce the hearts of many."

Stephanie remarked, "Obviously, in a good way. Lydia went over and threw the curtains open. She said, "It's so bright and beautiful outside. Not that it wasn't already, but now everyone is picking up paperwork and leaving."

Knowing Wisdom had presented an invitation, Stephanie said, "Wisdom, I do want to come to your house."

Wisdom's House

Immediately we were at Wisdom's house.

Stephanie remarked, "I see the wall again with all those pearls which represent people. We're sitting down and she has, for some reason, the most beautiful chocolate pie I have ever seen. She says that she knows I'm not too fond of meringue and there's no meringue on my pie. She is serving it to both of us. And I do not know why she's doing this, but I accept it. She said that sweets are Jesus' favorite thing! I honestly can't wait to get to Heaven and get some of that."

Wisdom said, "This is part of Him preparing a table before us in the presence of our enemies."

Stephanie remarked, "We get good things like this don't we?"

Wisdom said, "They don't even get the crumbs."

Wisdom continued, "Sit down; let me tell you a story." Three men were walking along a road. Each of them headed towards their destiny. They were on the same road, the same path, for a time. One stopped to see what was on the path, right at the edge. The others kept going, but he kept his attention on what was on the edge of this path. And, before too long, the two looked back and couldn't see him. They kept moving forward on their path. One of them met a beautiful young lady on the left side of the path. He knew he needed to keep going, but he stopped. The other man kept on walking but before he knew it, he could no longer see that second man when he looked back. He said to himself, "I'm alone walking on this path." And then, right in front of him were three separate pathways. He knew one was his, and the other two belonged to the other men behind him in the distance. He could see that all the paths led to the Kingdom of Heaven. He turned back anxiously to look for the other two men, and they were nowhere to be seen. He even thought about turning around and going to find them."

Then Wisdom turned and asked, "Which path would you take?"

Stephanie remarked, "Well, Wisdom, that was like a trick question because he looked ahead, and he could see (the three pathways) that they all ended up in the Kingdom of Heaven. I would take the path in front of him that was his all along, the straight path.

Stephanie stopped to think and then said, "Good point." Wisdom had said to her, "Did you inquire of me on which path to take?"

Stephanie replied, "I did not."

Wisdom remarked, "This is a mistake that many make, just like the first man who stopped to look at what was on the side of the road. He didn't inquire if it was something he should do. It kept him from moving forward. The young man that the beautiful woman stopped didn't ask me what he should do, and now is detained, and who knows for how long. The point is, at every turn, in everything, inquire of me. Wisdom is vital in these days. At every turn, in everything, inquire of me—Wisdom.

Stephanie commented, "I see, Wisdom, that there really wasn't a turn that he was going take but even in the moment of taking the next step, even (the next step) forward, he was to inquire of you. Thank you, Wisdom, for this reminder. It is profound. I ask that you remind me when I go to take a step or turn that I would inquire of you every time."

Wisdom said, "This is instruction for the masses. These are perilous times, and my presence is stronger than ever upon the earth because men have cried out to me."

Stephanie said, "We ask Wisdom, keep it ever before our face to inquire of you about everything."

Wisdom then exclaimed, "Now let's eat some pie!"

Stephanie remarked, "Okay, I'm down with that. Why did she put yours in a to-go box?"

Wisdom replied, "Well, Chocolate is not his favorite. It's Adina's favorite."

Stephanie exclaimed, "That's why it's in a to-go box! It's for her!

——— · ———

Chapter 24
The Kingdom Dynamic of Molecular Widgets

As we engaged Heaven this day, we found ourselves in a setting like the movie Avatar, where the main character, a paraplegic, climbs into a machine and becomes a body—an avatar.

We were not alone. Wisdom had come in high wisdom. Understanding had come in high understanding,[16] and now we were sitting with the council we have had before with all these participants. We could see Einstein, Moses, and Daniel here. We sat with them at the table in the room and waited.

Einstein stood, and started handing out devices he called widgets. He started passing them around to the group until everyone had one in front of them. He said,

---

[16] High Wisdom and High Understanding are levels of wisdom and understanding that are exceedingly uncommon.

"It is molecular." He began to tell us about this molecular widget—which is what he called it. Ezekiel came and touched each widget, bringing it to life.

Einstein said, "Consider the molecular structure."

The widget began flying right in front of us. It was fascinating. It looked like molecules put together in a three-dimensional piece, hovering.

Einstein asked, "If coming to this place truly turns back the hands of time. What would you say has happened to your molecular structure?"

Stephanie asked, "Are you referring to when we call for Jesus' DNA and RNA? Is that what you are talking about?"

"In some ways," he said.

We asked Wisdom and Understanding to take our hands and help us understand what this meant.

We know that everything has a molecular structure, and this is also about quantum.

Einstein surmised, "If everything has a molecular structure and everything is quantum, can you consider passing through these things?"

> *If everything has*
> *a molecular structure*
> *and everything is quantum,*
> *can you consider passing*
> *through these things?*

"When he said that, it was like we walked through a wall," Stephanie admitted.

He said, "I had to show you the form of a molecular widget for the sake of seeing. But you who are molecular, you are molecularly fashioned and can walk quantumly through molecularly fashioned things. For instance, walking on water. Walking through walls." The leaned in and said, "Walking through and on time."

Stephanie asked, "Can you tell us how or what are the next steps?"

Einstein asked, "Is your faith activated?"

"Yes, it is Einstein," she replied.

He said, "Then, walk through time."

We asked, "Will you come with us, Einstein?"

He said, "We can all come with you."

Stephanie described, "Immediately, I am seeing this entire scene change. I am seeing the time of my conception."

Einstein asked, "What if here we could change the molecular outcomes? The generational work that is at hand changes molecular outcomes. Does your faith sustain this?"

Stephanie replied, "Yes."

Einstein charged her, "Then change your molecular outcome."

She asked, "What are you talking about specifically? She then understood what to do next.

She said, "All right. I call in the molecular change into my body from my conception because of the work Jesus Christ has done for me because obedience is better than sacrifice. I have walked in this, and I stand on this timeline and say, 'I ask for the change in my molecular design back to perfection.'

She asked, "Are Jesus and the Father talking about healing bodies?"

He responded, "Healing in your bodies is one aspect of this."

Stephanie mentioned that she had had a lifelong hip issue. Einstein called it a 'hitch in her giddy up.'

She found herself on her timeline, walking back in it to the point of her conception. She stepped into that conception and could see the cells dividing. She announced, "From this place, because of the generational cleansing, because I have asked Jesus Christ for new DNA and RNA, I call in the molecular structure of Jesus into this moment in this place in Jesus' name."

She could hardly believe it was that simple and described what she was seeing as impurities being driven out.

When Jesus was speaking to his disciples, he said that the things he did, we would do those things and greater. Einstein said, "After the resurrection, did not Jesus appear to them? He walked into the room in front of Thomas and all of them."

Einstein said, "These are the next steps."

Daniel just stood, and he opened this book, and when he did, it was like lightning, or light came from the book and went straight up and covered the whole place.

Daniel said, "This is about elevation and the next level. This is the next level revelation."

We asked, "Why did it take Ezekiel touching it for the molecular widget to activate?"

Einstein explained, "Ezekiel wanted to be a part of the process."

They indicated these molecular widgets were something we could take with us, so we received them from Heaven.

Lydia, who had been with us, brought in a book. It was a leather-bound book tied with a red ribbon around it. Instead of opening it, she put it on a shelf, saying, "The old has passed away."

She pointed to the book on the table that Daniel had brought in and opened it. It signified a new revelation that had come.

We then called Ezekiel near and commissioned him, saying,

> *We commission you to use the molecular widgets to bring them to those who are doing and have done the generational work for the Kingdom. We commission you to the portals and to open wider the portals that need to be opened and to close those that need to be closed. Seal them shut with the blood of Jesus.*
>
> *I commission you to the flames and to the rightly dividing of the truth. Do this in time and out of time, and every dimension and realm, and co-labor with all the other angels of those that are part of this ministry in Jesus' name.*

More Understanding of the Widgets

Several days later, we engaged Heaven again to receive more understanding of these Molecular Widgets.

We met with Einstein and asked, "What do you want to share with us?"

He asked, "What is molecular?"

We responded, "It relates to or consists of molecules. It involves the interactions between polymer and solvent at the molecular level. A molecule is a group of two or more atoms held together by attractive forces known as chemical bonds." (Wikipedia)

We had been taken to a cliff overlooking an ocean moments before, but now, things looked quite different once the definition of molecular had been read. We saw the scenery now as lines, prisms, planes, numbers, and what we assumed were molecules.

Einstein said, "Everything—all of creation is molecular."

All of creation is molecular.

We asked, "What are molecular widgets?"

He called it a download.

We asked, "Is this something that you are saying we can request just for the sake of learning?"

He said, "Heaven is giving you this ease, this simplicity of requesting something. It is a connection because the expanse of everything is molecular. You are molecular. It is an integration."

Our understanding of a widget is that it is something that can be embedded. Stephanie had experienced this embedding a few days before when Einstein suddenly took the widget he held in his hand and placed it in Stephanie's mind. As she looked at her hand, she could see all kinds of molecular constructs embedded inside of her.

He said, "This is already within. Heaven has given you the bandwidth for it. Heaven had me give you a visual picture of implanting the molecular widget in your mind for your mind to expand. It was a way for your soul to understand that you would see something.

"You are molecular; you are integrated, so think bigger."

Seeing the widget in her hand again, Stephanie asked that it be embedded in her. This time, instead of being embedded in her mind, it was embedded in her heart.

Immediately she felt drawn to everything that she had seen of the ocean and the sky. She felt her heart pull to it as if a part of it now. She could go and be in the water or be in the beauty of the sky. It was integrated in her where we were. It was like being one with the creation around her.

Einstein said, "The widget is for the sake of understanding. To create an ease."

"Can we ask this for people?" We wanted to know.

We suddenly saw an expanse of angels with widgets in their hands.

He said, "It is a tool for your vision to know that you have this and that you have access to it. Some need to see this for themselves as an action."

Stephanie remarked, "As an act of faith, Einstein, I ask for all the molecular widgets that Heaven would have for Ron and for me.

She continued, "He just showed me that the book of LifeSpring—the entity—is molecular. It did not look like a book anymore. Even though we could see pages, it was molecular. The book is in you, Ron. It is in me. My heart is drawn to become a living part of it."

Einstein said, "As we begin to view your integration around you, that you are a part of these things—all of creation—you will be able to understand governing better. Because if you are in union with Him, you will realize that you are a part of creation, and creation is a part of you. You are integrated because he made all of this. You can go and govern the sea or the land you are standing on. You can govern a tree, or you can govern whatever it is around you.

"The widget is for the sake of just the visual. It is an embedding in people who want to see and experience that embedding for the sake of the expansion of their mind and heart."

Stephanie added, "I am guessing that I just would not have been able to have grasped these things without the widget being embedded. Because when he planted it in my head, I had no problem seeing something outside of my norm because I knew it was a heavenly implant that wasn't anything I could produce."

Einstein finished, saying, "Rest in this. Now govern."

We asked, "May we ask for molecular widgets on behalf of the people for tonight for it to be an activation?"

In response, Stephanie could suddenly see Ezekiel's ranks with widgets in their hands. Each of them looked different. They were very uniquely designed for each person because each person is unique. Each person will have something specific and different from the person next to them. But in the same sense, it is as if it is still the same.

We were told, "What they are receiving is individualized oneness, which is an oxymoron."

———·———

Chapter 25
The Kingdom Dynamic of Freedom from Fragility

On a recent engagement with Heaven, Wisdom met us holding a single daisy. We discussed the fragility of the daisies, and Wisdom began to teach us about the power of the restoration of Innocence. In the recent book Kingdom Dynamics – Volume 1, we shared about the pink capture bags and how they restore innocence in our lives. Originally, all of us stood before the Father in Innocence. However, through the events of life, Innocence gets stolen from us. Sometimes bit by bit, other times in large chunks, it seems.

Wisdom said,

When innocence is restored, fragility is broken.

"When a bouquet of daisies and wind comes, they are not as easily broken. They are not so fragile."

Wisdom explained to us, "In the true innocence of where you stood before God, all was given to you at that moment before you touched the earth. He gave mankind everything. There was no fragileness in His creation. Restoring innocence brings strength to the body (not just an individual, but to the Body of Christ). "When there is innocence and intimacy between a son and his father, the restoration of innocence can occur in a blink of an eye."

"When there's innocence and intimacy between a son and his father if, in no other manner that people know how to restore innocence for themselves by standing before the Father and asking for Innocence to be restored, in that intimacy, it can be done in a blink of an eye."

Stephanie remarked, "Wisdom, the feeling I am getting about Innocence and the restoration of it upon a person, is the strength it brings because all of what happened with 'as if it never were.' Because before innocence was restored, the person deals with all the frailties, and brokenness, but the restoration of Innocence is like a bonding. I am seeing it like a super glue of some sort."

Wisdom replied, "You can learn spirit-forward and even having the Glory rise up, *but until Innocence is fully restored, there will be a fragility.* Intimacy and innocence restored will bond the strength.

> *You are truly to stand with one foot in Heaven and one foot on the earth.*

Stephanie then shared a story from the prior evening at a Bible study group she attends. "When we had our prayer meeting last night, we stood up, asked the Glory to rise, and stepped into the Spirit of Excellence. As we did, I saw that line down the middle of my body. I turned, so I had Heaven down my right side and earth down my left. And the Lord said, 'What do you think about the right brain versus the left brain?' I know that the right brain involves creativity and your spirit."

Wisdom asked, "Did you enjoy walking in both realms today at your office?"

Stephanie replied, "I did enjoy that. I enjoyed walking into the office today with one foot in Heaven and one foot on earth; it was easier. There was a strength."

As Stephanie was talking, Wisdom handed her a tool belt. With it came the understanding that the things we were learning were tools to walk this out in our daily lives.

Wisdom said, "I built my house with those tools."

Chapter 26

The Kingdom Dynamic of the Expanse of the Kingdom

Stephanie said, "I'm on a glass elevator, and Lydia is with me. Hi Lydia. I can see the different floors of this building, and this time Lydia said, we're going all the way to the top."

Stephanie asked, "Lydia, what's on the top?"

We exited the elevator, and from the rooftop, Lydia said, "See the expanse of the Kingdom."

Stephanie perceived that she was referring to our ministry on earth. "Lydia, are you telling me that we're expanding?"

Lydia again said, "Do you see the expanse of the Kingdom?"

Stephanie replied, "Okay, Lydia, I say 'yes.' I see the expanse of the Kingdom as an act of faith. I choose to see it. Ron chooses to see what this is."

Then, everything we had been looking at in Heaven came in fast. We were now looking at four walls around us.

Lydia commanded, "Break down the barriers of the wall before you."

Stephanie felt like she was supposed to kick it down, so she did. She turned to the next wall. She knew she was to use angelic assistance this time. She called Ezekiel, his commanders, ranks, and patrollers to come near. Then she said, "Ezekiel, I commission you to remove this wall." Immediately, they pulled it down. Then she turned to the next wall.

Lydia directed, "Speak the word."

Stephanie declared, "I speak the word that no weapon formed against LifeSpring International Ministries shall prosper, and every tongue that rises against it is already condemned."

The wall flew back and flew away.

She turned to the next wall, the last one, and asked, "How are we to take this wall down?"

Lydia replied, "His Kingdom come."

Stephanie said, "I speak, His Kingdom come, His will be done on earth as it is in Heaven."

Ezekiel then came and just put one foot on it, and it fell over with his foot still on it. Then he stood on it.

Lydia said, "The four walls that were considered the church will no longer be the same, feel the same or look the same." She snapped her finger, and Lydia said again, "See the expanse of the Kingdom."

Stephanie said, "I'm turning now and seeing the expanse of LifeSpring. I see different people. People that work for us in offices."

Lydia remarked, "See, the seed has multiplied."

Stephanie began seeing several of our team members and saw a root system—how the roots of a plant would grow. The team members were at the top, above it all, with the root system below, and there were more people.

We got back on the elevator, got off on one of the floors and entered a conference room. Malcolm was with Einstein, Peter, Moses, Wisdom, John, and King David."

Malcolm said, "This is a forum."

We were seated at the table, and some of our heavenly advisory team was also present with us.

Malcolm said, "This is a meeting of the minds. A planning commission—inter-networking."

Moses stood with fire in his eyes and proclaimed, "His name is great and greatly to be praised. The Bond of Excellence has been upon you. You are forerunners, but you are not just forerunners in name only, but in deed, the magnified multiplied Word of the Lord is coming from this mountain."

Stephanie remarked, "No wonder they would use Moses since he had been on a mountain. Thank you, Moses."

Moses said, "See that you hold to the Word of the Lord—not only to what is coming, but what is here and now—what is present.

Stephanie asked, "Moses, what do we do to forerun, not just in name, but in deed?"

Moses replied, "Indeed you shall forerun for you have been called *Makers of the Way*. Justice is at His right hand. The courts are expanding."

Stephanie noted that when he said this a gavel came down. He sat down, and Wisdom stood. John the Baptist stood at the same time. They came together, linked arms elbow to elbow and stood on the conference table together."

Wisdom said, "Link arms, link arms."

Stephanie commented, "Wisdom, I don't even pretend to know or understand, but I know you have given us the Spirit of Understanding and Knowledge, so help me, us, to know what this is. What are we linking arms with or to whom?"

Wisdom said, "Link arms to the host of Heaven."

Stephanie said, "We say yes, and we ask to link arms with the host of Heaven."

Wisdom added, "Your faith has been proven."

"You, Ron, have led the people into understanding co-laboring with angels. Linking arms is a strategy."

Stephanie added, "Well, we say, in the name of Jesus, that we link arms with the host of Heaven. We commission the host of Heaven to link arms with us. The last time I said the word 'arms,' they became like weapons. These are decrees with the angels' words, which are weapons."

Wisdom added, "The weapons of your warfare are not carnal but mighty through the pulling down of strongholds."[17]

Stephanie asked, "Wisdom, is there a specific linking of arms with the host? Are there words that become weapons?"

Wisdom replied, "See the expanse of the kingdom."

Stephanie began a commissioning:

We commission the angels, the host of Heaven, as we link arms with them, to link arms with all those who come near, draw near, and are a part of LifeSpring and their families. For those who are a part of LifeSpring International Ministries and the entity of it and all the expanse of it. We commission you to help us see the expanse of the Kingdom. To see the expanse of the Kingdom and for it to be seen in Jesus' name.

---

[17] 2 Corinthians 10:4

Now she and John the Baptist have gotten down off the table. Mark is here, and he stood up.

Mark began, "Mark my words: transition."

Stephanie asked, "Did you say transition is coming or is here?"

Mark replied, "It's now. Transition yourselves for the intake. It does not violate the word, but intake is now. It's an action word—intake. Those from the left and the right, intake the seed and the harvest—intake."

Stephanie could then see Alicia writing names and realized that someone in the room had been speaking names, and she had been writing them down. These were the names of individuals.

Stephanie said, "I'm putting two and two together that Alicia is our Personnel Advisor, and she is writing down people's names to be a part of the ministry. Einstein just handed me a light bulb, and when he handed it to me, the light came on."

Einstein added, "Take in the aha moments, for they are of the Lord, and He alone will receive praise."

Stephanie remarked, "I keep hearing the words 'thoughts' and 'processes.' I commission the angels to the thoughts and processes—the aha moments."

Einstein showed her people trying to understand the Courts of Heaven or any of the books LifeSpring has published. Some have had trouble, and that will change, and they will experience light bulb moments of clarity—removal of the hindrances.

The Plan of Action

Stephanie continued, "There are books that Lydia has put in front of us that say *Plan of Action*." Stephanie paused to see if she could open it and read it. There is a light bulb above each one of them that's on. There's a wind coming in right now. It's gentle, but it's enough to turn the page to open this Plan of Action. I'm watching a hand sign the name of the Lord Jesus Christ to the plan. Holy Spirit is doing this to this action plan."

Lydia said, "This provision has been made for this Plan of Action, not by might, not by power, but by my spirit, says the Lord. It is sufficient for you."

Jesus came into the room and starting at the far end of the table from us embracing and greeting each person around the table. He came to us, and took His hand, and put it on the *Plan of Action* book. He has His hand upon this work. He walked Stephanie to Ron and took Ron's hand, lifted it, and placed His hand on Ron's—palm to palm.

Jesus said, "Eye has not seen, ear has not heard."

Stephanie continued, "Now He has left the room, and the light bulbs suspended above all the books have sunk into the books, illuminating them even though the books have closed. Lydia is taking the books, which she stacked one on top of the other.

"The understanding I'm having is each person at this table has put that thing that was a representation of what they are adding to this expanse—their addition of what they are bringing to the table and what they have brought to the table. Alicia is taking with her the book that has the names."

Lydia then said, "Come with me."

We began following her, and she stopped to give all the books to Ezekiel, but a second copy of them went to the Court of Records. Our scribes are taking them and opening them up. There were many scribes, and each scribe had a book. Each was assigned a book, and each scribe took their pieces and put them in a blender and blended all of them together. They are blending everything that each person has brought to the table. It is now one very large book. On the front, you could still see the imprint of the hand of Jesus.

The book then went into our vault, which is why George is here. George then pulled coins, gold bricks and tons of cash out and put them into the ministries ATM."

George said to me, "You have full access."

While George was putting the money and other things into the ATM, he sang, "...leaving on a jet plane, don't know when I'll be back again...."

———·———

Chapter 27
The Kingdom Dynamic of Serendipity

This engagement with Heaven started with the phrase, "We are excited to know what Heaven has."

Stephanie began describing the scene, "I immediately saw the entity with the shofar who we've seen before, and we step in to know what your heart is about this, Father. Jesus, thank you for being the way we step into Heaven. I see trumpeters and those blowing shofars. They are far from me. We have seen these entities before. I can't hear the sound, but I see the sound.

"Hey Malcolm, can you tell me what's going on?

"Hey, Wisdom," Stephanie said. "Wisdom just came up to my right."

Wisdom said, "Rejoice, rejoice, rejoice! The word of the Lord has gone forth and broken through. Many shall see this light, the dawning of the new day."

Stephanie replied, "Oh, they said that the other day too."

Wisdom remarked, "The conflict in the spirit has been brought low. Serendipity."

Stephanie asked, "What does 'serendipity' mean?"

I explained, "Serendipity is an unplanned, fortunate discovery."

Stephanie added, "A phenomenon of finding valuable or agreeable things not sought for. We thank you, Father, for serendipity. It is in the spirit. I feel it. Thank you, Heaven. Thank you, Father. We rejoice with Heaven. We rejoice that conflict has been brought low. That serendipity is the move forward."

Wisdom said, "There are causeways, fountain ways, truth ways, and waves upon waves upon waves of this phenomenon. This is unmatchable. This is unspeakable to human understanding, but the spirit rejoices, the spirit is in agreement."

Malcolm remarked, "You will taste and see that the Lord is good. You will not look in the natural at a hindrance. Look at it as a means to an end. What's coming will meet the means. Arise that your light might shine. This is a new day."

Stephanie continued, "Now I'm looking at where all those beings were blowing the trumpets and shofars. It's not a scattering, but there is movement. They blew the trumpets, and they're moving forward in the spirit.

Malcolm explained, "They are moving into their pre-vortex of time ordained by the Lord, commissioned on behalf of the sons, on behalf of His work.

Stephanie remarked, "Ezekiel is here. He's trying to show me something in his hand; Ezekiel, what is in your hand? It's a small piece of paper in a perfect square. Do I open it? What do I do with this perfect square? Is there some meaning, mathematically, to a perfect square? There's a reason that it's a perfect square."

I paused to look up a definition of a perfect square and found, 'Perfect square numbers are not only limited to the numerals, but also in algebraic definitions.'

Stephanie said, "Well, we take this perfect square outside our understanding as you unravel it. Malcolm is having me open the square! As I open this up to revelation knowledge, we say 'yes' to whatever this square is in the spirit.

Ezekiel (who had appeared) said, "For such a time as this."

Stephanie responded, "For such a time as this.'

Father, I ask on behalf of Ezekiel, his commanders, and ranks. We commend him, his commanders, and ranks to you, and his patrollers, and his protective detail for the saints. We request angel food, bread, and elixir of every number and flavor. I request the lasso. (Ezekiel) is showing me that he has already used the lasso and needs a new one. I request marching orders for Ezekiel, in the name of Jesus.

Ezekiel, we commission the full use of these instruments of war and illumination from the light in the name of Jesus on behalf of LifeSpring.

"Wisdom, I can't help but feel excited about today. You've mentioned the dawning of a new day, and we're excited to know more."

Wisdom replied, "It is as Ezekiel has said, 'for such a time as this,'"

Stephanie prayed,

We thank you, Father. We say, Your Kingdom come, and Your will be done on earth as it is in Heaven. Thank you for that song, "Great is thy faithfulness," that just came in my mind. We thank you, Father, that great is Your faithfulness. Great is your faithfulness to Ron and Adina. Great is your faithfulness to the family. Great is your faithfulness to me and all those that have joined LifeSpring.

She remarked, "That is interesting wisdom."

Wisdom noted, "Isn't it interesting that all of this falls around Ron's 65th birthday?"

I remarked, "Now, to help you understand a perfect square number. Twenty-five is a perfect square because five times five equals 25. Sixteen is a perfect square, because four times four is 16. That type of number is a perfect square."

Stephanie commented, "What does it mean for us or this work? The square was for something because it was a tiny, perfect square in his big hand, but he had me open it, and so I did, and it doubled. I just got that when I opened it up, it doubled as another perfect square."

———·———

Chapter 28
The Kingdom Dynamic of Ruling as a Son

But you are God's chosen treasure—priests who are kings, a spiritual "nation" set apart as God's devoted ones. He called you out of darkness to experience his marvelous light, and now he claims you as his very own. He did this so that you would broadcast his glorious wonders worldwide.

¹⁰ For at one time you were not God's people, but now you are. At one time you knew nothing of God's mercy, because you hadn't received it yet, but now you are drenched with it! (1 Peter 2:9-10) (TPT)

The Mirror Bible reads,

> *⁹ You are proof of the authentic generation. You give testimony to the original idea of the royalty of true priesthood. The order of Melchizedek, you are a perfect prototype of the mass of humanity. You are the generation of people who exhibit the*

conclusion of the prophetic poetic thoughts. Thought of God that has come full circle. You published the excellence of his elevation and display that your authentic identity has been rescued out of obscurity and brought into a spectacular light. ¹⁰ *You were once a people without identity, but have now discovered the integrity of your original identity in God, where there was no mercy. You have now received much mercy. (THE MIRROR)*

As we engaged Heaven, we were referred to this passage of Scripture. We had heard the phrase "Kings and Priests" moments before. Upon reading the Scriptures, we heard Enoch, who looked at us and plainly said,

---
Rule. Tell the people to rule.

"If they have obtained mercy and grace through Jesus, why shouldn't they rule?

In 1 Peter 2:25, it says we are completely vulnerable, just like sheep roaming astray without direction or protection. But now we have returned and are restored to the shepherd and guardian of our souls.

Rule. Govern your territory.

> *Do not permit wickedness to rule
> because you have the right to govern.*

You are a son and because you understand that position, you become the reigning spiritual authority in that territory for that purpose. Stand in your place, rule from where you are and say, "Not in my territory! Not on my watch! Not in my town!"

In the film *The Lord of the Rings: The Return of the King*, there is a scene that shows someone giving Aragon a sword. They say to him, "Become who you were born to be!" In becoming who *we* are born to be, *we rule and reign as sons*, because *we were born to become sons*-kings and priests.

Before you can rule, however…

> *You must become
> who you were born to be
> and learn to stand in that place.*

We have done a lot of work teaching about sonship. We were told to embolden ourselves. The next step is where we stand up and step into our place as a son.

Chapter 29
The Kingdom Dynamic
of a Quieted & Enlarged Soul

David Porter and I were introduced to the Library of Revelation during a recent engagement with Heaven. The amount of revelation available in that place within the realms of Heaven is hard to fathom. Our souls were having trouble assimilating what was being presented.

David, who only in the last year or so had learned about calling his spirit forward and telling his soul to relax and stand down, was sensing the resistance of his soul.

On one occasion a few months ago, he had given those instructions, and he heard his soul say, "I know! I know," as it conceded and stepped back, allowing his spirit to come forward.

David, the psalmist, described this in Psalms 131:1-3.

Lord, my heart is meek before you. I don't consider myself better than others. I'm content to not pursue matters that are over my head—such as your complex mysteries and wonders—that I'm not yet ready to understand.

² I am humbled and quieted in your presence. Like a contented child who rests on its mother's lap, I'm your resting child and **my soul is content in you.**

³ O people of God, your time has come to quietly trust, waiting upon the Lord now and forever. (TPT)

As David Porter and I were in the engagement, I was instructed to tell him to enlarge his soul. I advised him to perform a prophetic act of pressing against the sides of his soul to stretch it as you would if you were inside a giant balloon and were attempting to stretch it out by pressing it with your hands. He did these motions in several directions—side to side, corner to corner, top to bottom. As he did so, he felt an ease come into his soul to grasp the information he was receiving from Heaven more easily.

We have taught this same process to others, and they have experienced the same ease. They also have experienced an increase in the love of the Father for others. Others have testified of increased patience with people, while others have noted their spirit's ability to cooperate more with what is being downloaded from Heaven.

We have been taught that our soul is our enemy and an enemy of our ability to fulfill the will of God in our lives when that is not the case. It is not our enemy. It is the interface between realms. It helps our body receive what is occurring in it as what comes from Heaven passes through our spirit to our soul and finally to our body. It simply needs some training in what to do and clarity in its job description.

Job Description of the Soul:

- Be a bridge from our spirit to our body.
- Not be a gatekeeper concerning the things sent from Heaven.
- Not trying to figure out everything—it is not its job. Solutions come from Heaven, not from the soul realm.
- Not trying to figure out revelation.
- Not to be the first landing place for revelation.
- To help the spirit in delivering from Heaven to our physical body.

Chapter 30
The Kingdom Dynamic of Letting the Glory Stand Up

As we engaged Heaven this day, several things were occurring simultaneously. We had explicitly engaged for instructions on behalf of Sandhills Ecclesia, but Heaven had other things in mind.

David sensed Albert enter the room where he was, and I noticed that Albert was accompanied by at least one other being. David asked who it was and was told Ezekiel, the prophet, had come.

Ezekiel reminded us not to think it strange that we were seeing him and other men and women in white as we have learned to engage them. We have welcomed and made room for them, so they are showing up.

We must make room for engagements with the men and women in white.

It pleases the Father when we learn how to accurately and skillfully engage the dynamics of His Glory and His Kingdom. While on earth, Albert experienced seeing the Glory of God many times. It was now his assignment to tutor us.

I also sensed that he would have things to teach David Porter, concerning the Glory. David then announced, "Enoch is here."

Enoch was one of the two men that went to Heaven without dying. He became a relocated spirit. Elijah was the other one, who was caught up in the whirlwind (portal).

We began to walk with them, and speaking to David, Enoch said, "My son, many questions will be answered. Many revelations will be unpacked and released. David, this is an answer to your prayer. You have longed to know about this. You are now ready.

"Your journey has been long, but it has been intentional. The church here in the Sandhills[18] is to be one of many to first partake of the realms of Glory, not just to go in and out, but to walk and live in the Glory, to maintain, to occupy, to rest, and to operate from the Glory as mature sons, for many shall mature quickly. Some will mature gradually, but it's the Father's heart's cry, and intent to bring *all* sons into *maturity*.

---

[18] Sandhills Ecclesia (SandhillsEcclesia.com), one of the extensions of LifeSpring.

"This realm, this place, this plane is obtainable. I am a witness, for many read in the Scriptures about my experience. Still those experiences were not even the tip of the iceberg, as you would say, for there are many things that are not written in the Scriptures that I have experienced, that I have come to teach you. It is my assignment. My brother, Ezekiel, and I are both assigned to you, for the Sandhills region shall be changed. There shall be a remarkable, tangible, recognizable change in your region, world, and even the land you occupy. Sandhills is not just an earthly geographical plane; it has been given global and heavenly authority. It is the extension of the Kingdom of God. So are the citizens and servants of the most high God. More men and women in white linen have been waiting to serve. Now come and walk with me.

Your spirits are already enlightened and aware of this existence.

"And as you have practiced living spirit-forward, it has afforded you the grace, the love of the Father and the fruit. The seeds that you have planted are now evident, for you shall be equippers. You are part of the last-day revolution and expanding of the Kingdom of God on the earth.

You have wondered what it is like to be translated. As you walk with me, with Ezekiel, and as you continue to be faithful in this, the Father will open more portals of His Glory to you, so be attentive to every instruction."

David began to see the Golden Pathway before him. People[19] were on both sides of it cheering us on.

Stephanie added, "I know there are a lot of people here. I have been in the background. Gail's been walking with me while you were in the foreground. There is the path we are walking on which you were speaking about. There are two portals at which they[20] have stopped. The two portals are side by side and a little bit overlapping. The two men have taken something and placed it at the overlapping point, where the two points meet at the bottom. I am trying to get a visual of what it is, but they buried it there. It's a foundational timepiece of some sort, a substance that is allowing these portals to stay open. This is what David and Ron will pass through."

Enoch turned and said, "You are right, sister. This is for this time right now. And when that time is over, these portals are going to close. But right now, the time is now."

Stephanie remarked, "They're telling us, Ron, as you and I call Lydia forward or call others forward, we can step into this place and say we want to meet with Ezekiel and Enoch."

I asked, "What should I share with the folks on Sunday? What do you recommend, gentlemen?"

Stephanie intoned, "Well, the sense that I am getting is that it is preparation time leading up to the conference.

---

[19] The Cloud of Witnesses of Hebrews 12:1
[20] Enoch and Ezekiel

Something is going to happen at that meeting that is unique and different. I know that not everyone that is in Sandhills Ecclesia will be at the conference, but this revelation has something to do with the revelation of the Glory.

"This is a time where the timepiece put at the base of the portals will work to allow the sons to walk through. It will be open for now.

"Gail, I keep seeing you. You have been walking with me, and these men are up front. Is there anything specific? You are trying to highlight something to me.

Gail said, "The sons need to know their faithful stewarding of the human spirit, the joint unity, walking in the knowledge that they can walk in it daily, from this point forward, because 'where much is received much is required,' but because of their faithfulness in it, they need to know that all of Heaven, the Enochs, the Elijahs, the Peters, the Pauls and the Moseses are available to them, but they must walk in it. They must step in, know, and believe, as John the Baptist said when he revealed that he is a son just like we are sons and that there is no celebrity status in Heaven, except for Jesus. Know you are sons. There is much revelation to be given to the body."

Stephanie added, "This is available to them. That timepiece is specifically for Enoch and Elijah. I do not know, but we will have the opportunity to engage with them all the time—the ministry is.

Enoch interjected, "Yes, because you are seasoned, you grow by leaps and bounds, and it is not past tense. It is continual."

Stephanie repeated what she had just heard, "We grow every day by leaps and bounds in our faith."

David asked, "What does the number seven mean?" Adina replied, "Completion."

Stephanie added, "Also, restoration. Also, today is the seventh of July, the 7th month.

David said, "Wow. It also has been seven months since we started in January. I know at this moment; I feel engulfed in the Glory."

Stephanie declared, "Ron, there will be some downloads for you. David, you will have a word that both men will give you.

"I just thought of that Scripture about how Elisha said to Elijah, 'I want a double portion of your anointing.' I personally (and I know David, Ron, and Adina do, too) want that too! I'm like, me too! Standing here, I want it all the time.

"Enoch has a fireball in his hand, and David, he is plunging it into your chest. He is putting it right in there."

Enoch remarked, "That should ignite something." David replied, "Thank you."

Ezekiel said, "The church of the firstborn has grown in numbers because of this work in this ministry."

Stephanie said, "I'm assuming he's referring to last Sunday when we conducted a mass transition of LHS's."

Enoch and Ezekiel said,

> *Walking in the glory is not an event. It is an expression and manifestation of what it is to live Heaven down.*

Ezekiel said, "Mirror us."

Stephanie's vision ended, but David was still receiving a download. He said, "The glory is the release and the authority of the sons, your birthright, your inheritance. Now, are you the sons of God now?

"This is not futuristic in theory. This is reality—the reality that has been hidden, but now is being released."

Stephanie remarked, "It is part of the book of Daniel being opened. It is another part of 'walking on water.' When we call our spirit forward, we were told about having our spirit forward and it being the bubble around the body. But the Glory stands up to walk on water. You must have your spirit forward, and the Glory, it must stand up. I cannot wait to walk on some water. I will be out on this gulf (the Gulf of Mexico, right outside her condominium window where she was vacationing).

At Ron's prompting, David asked about the passage in Ezekiel where the Glory of the Lord stood up. He said, I would like to ask Heaven to share with us about the Glory of the Lord standing up."

Ezekiel said, "Do you remember in the Scriptures where the evangelist was moved from one place to another?[21] Do you remember in Scripture how Jesus moved through the crowd? How hard is this? It is not hard at all."

David said, "So what question should I ask? What question should I ask you?"

Stephanie enjoined, "I know. They showed me that those who are filled with the Holy Spirit are indwelt, right? We have an indwelling of the Holy Spirit that rises up. That Glory rises up inside of us through our spirit-man. That is what stands up in us, specifically. I was sitting there thinking, 'are you telling me that those of us who are spirit-filled, who understand being spirit forward can have the Glory stand up?'"

I asked, "So how do we maximize that?"

Ezekiel said, "You all have experienced it already: Adina, when she plays music. Ron, when you teach, Stephanie, when you see and sing, David, when you minister or prophesy, you have experienced it already."

Stephanie added, "I can see it. I see a futuristic piece of me standing next to Ron and David. Kevin is standing there, and I see the Glory stand up—rise. At first, it's seated when I am soul forward but then I bring my spirit forward, and I ask for the Glory to stand up in me, and it stands. It is bigger. Obviously, it is taller than I am

---

[21] Acts 8:34-40

because it is not me. It dwells in me because I am spirit-filled and understand being spirit-forward."

David repeated, "How do we maximize it?"

Enoch and Elijah said, "Practice releasing, speaking, moving. It is just like breathing." Stephanie said to Ron, "Ron, ask for the Glory to stand up inside of you right now."

I said, "Glory, stand up. Stand up."

Stephanie remarked, "Glory, stand up! Oh, I feel like we are ninety feet tall!"

Stephanie added, "This is Christ in us. The hope of Glory."

David remarked, "I have experienced this before, but I did not have a label for it." Stephanie said, "The hope of Glory! This is Jesus Christ dwelling in us as we have asked Glory to stand up, and this is the hope of Glory. We hoped for it. Now we have it!

"Oh, my goodness. We can surely stand on that mountain top now because I feel ninety feet tall, reigning, and governing with the Glory standing up inside of me! Wow!"[22]

---

[22] As I called for the Glory to stand up within me, I had the sensation of my skin stretching—not unlike the depiction of the Marvel Comics character, The Incredible Hulk, who goes from a normal sized man to a much larger being in a matter of seconds.

David said, "It is a spiritual reality. That is how we maximize it. Just like you have become comfortable in living spirit-first—spirit-forward. You do this in the same manner—just do it. You just do it!"

Stephanie commented, "Just do it! Christ in us, the hope of Glory. Wow. It takes the pressure off anybody who listens to this. They don't have to do anything! This is Him standing up! The One who is in us.

David remarked, "I do not know if I want to call this an epiphany, but I just saw that our soul, body, and spirit are already aware of what it means. You have been doing it, but you have not been aware that that is what you have been doing. Every time we call our spirit forward, we release the Glory. We just have not verbalized it in that manner.

Stephanie added, "But now we are telling ourselves something different, Enoch and Elijah are telling us to stand up. It is additional info!

"During this time, they have had to teach us to come forward, spirit-forward, and now we're going to be standing up because of the knowledge that Christ is IN US, the HOPE OF GLORY—STANDING UP!"

David commented, "What I have been saying is, 'I release the Glory. I release the Glory. I release the Glory,' at different intervals, at various times in the store, or in the car. I just felt to release the Glory here, released the Glory there, release the Glory at home. I just release the Glory."

Stephanie said, "Now you'll stand up, and you'll feel it stand up when you call it to stand up."

David added, "We were directed two weeks ago when Adina said, 'Come out of the cave.'"

"That was loaded. That was loaded. It was not just us coming out of the cave. This is what Ezekiel was saying, 'Come all the way out. Abandon what you have been used to and just come forth. Stand up, Glory, stand up. We have been saying Glory, come, Glory, come."

I interjected, "The Glory is *in* us!"

———·———

Chapter 31
The Kingdom Dynamic of the Spirit of Excellence

Stephanie remarked, "I just keep hearing the 'Spirit of excellence' and then, 'His name is great and greatly to be praised.' This encounter is about Noah because I've been walking along this mountainous ridgeline while looking down at the water and what looks like the boat that was Noah's. This is about the "Spirit of Excellence" and Noah.

"I'm seeing this boat travel in the water, and as I'm watching it; the waves are getting a little rougher and rougher as it goes. What's remarkable is that I'm still on this ridge, and My spirit man is keeping up with the boat.

"I'm interested in this boat and the message around the 'Spirit of Excellence.'"

Seth was our teacher, and we asked, "What about the Spirit of Excellence are you wanting to tell us?"

Seth asked, "Do you remember how many days it took to build this boat?"

Adina replied, "Like 120 years or something. It was a long time."

Seth continued, "Do you think that there was excellence involved?"

Stephanie answered, "Yes."

Seth asked, "Why?"

Stephanie responded, "Well, the boat needed to be watertight for one."

Seth continued his query, "In the Spirit of Excellence, how many lessons do you think Noah learned?"

Stephanie remarked, "Well, according to what I'm seeing with this boat, in building the boat, he learned quite a lot because it was waterproof and he had to prepare for every animal, and also, it was more than just the 40 days and 40 nights that he was on that boat."

Seth asked, "Do you think everyone on board walked in the Spirit of Excellence as he did?"

Stephanie replied, "I'm not sure, but I would say no."

Seth commented, "What a valuable lesson they learned by watching him walk it out. The Spirit of Excellence is a concrete thing."

Stephanie asked, "When you say 'concrete, I know the gist of what you're saying, but concrete stands out to me. What is specific about that word?"

Seth posed, "The Spirit of Excellence stands up."

Stephanie remarked, "Are you telling me that we can ask the Spirit of Excellence to stand up in us as we do the Glory?"

Seth asked (shrugging his shoulders), "Why not?"

Stephanie immediately said, "Okay, let's do it. I first ask for the Glory to stand up in me, and now I ask for the Spirit of Excellence to stand up as concrete.

"For me, it's a knowing of assurance. It's such a knowing of assurance of everything."

David interjected, "While you talked a little bit ago, I heard 'building—build.' Build according to the pattern, and because Noah built according to the pattern, the boat was concrete in how it was built, formed, and designed in every way. And no matter what happened on the outside, it maintained its existence because of how it was built. Even today, adventurers were able to discover it. The foundation is solid."

Stephanie said, "I see Noah standing in the Spirit of Excellence as such a solid figure. To take so many years to build something and not give up, even when people come against you, takes the Spirit of Excellence. We get mad when someone comes against us even once. He did it for years and walked in the concrete, solid knowledge and assurance of what would come. That's how he was able to bear it."

Adina added, "He maintained the vision and the Spirit of Excellence."

Seth leaned up against a tree with his arms crossed and smiled.

David continued, "He continued the vision despite opposition, chatter, and disbelief."

Stephanie interjected, "And every demonic force that would come against him. He and his family were the only ones saved in the storm. No one else was deemed worthy because of the demonic activity in their lives. Here we are today, and we have some opposition, and we cry like babies.

"This man stood in the Spirit of Excellence—his spirit man stood in the Spirit of Excellence. His spirit became excellent in these things for him to endure. Who are we to say anything about anything? We must call our spirit man to excellence, to walk in it these days.

"When I told my spirit to stand up and walk in excellence, I felt such an assurance of who I was, of who God is. And no matter what, I experienced the authority. It wasn't even an 'everything's going to be okay' assurance. It was an assurance I have never experienced before.

Adina asked, "How did Noah walk through this? He walked with his spirit forward. He didn't shrink back. What I see is with all the opposition, even with the eight souls with him, that means some extended family didn't believe."

Put your heart and soul into every activity you do, as though you are doing it for the Lord himself and not merely for others. (Colossians 3:23) (TPT)

Whatever you do, picture Christ in the person you're doing it for. It makes such a difference when you put your heart into it. (Colossians 3:23) (MIRROR)

Stephanie added, "To live contrary to the life of your design is to injure yourself. Well, Seth, I'm always interested in the 'one who is telling about this engagement' and the 'why'."

Seth is a man in white, and he wants to show us the reason why."

Ron added, "In the note to Romans 8:32 (MIRROR), Paul said, 'sin left mankind with an enormous shortfall; grace restores mankind to *excellence*."

Stephanie shared, "The image I keep seeing is that Seth was in the Roman era, and he was in an arena and going to be fed to the lions. The Spirit of Excellence he walked in landed him in there, but he never wavered."

She asked Seth, "Can you show me more? I see you in the arena, and I see that you literally have no fear."

Seth replied, "It took me a long time to figure out who I was. But once I did, it didn't take me long to figure out that walking in the Spirit of Excellence was the only way to live, even if it meant to die. Do you feel the strength and the authority in that?"

Stephanie replied, "When I tell my spirit to come forward, and I stand in the concreteness of the Spirit of Excellence, yes, I do."

Seth added, "Why live any other way?"

Stephanie said, "Seth, I'm going to ask you a practical question. How long did it take you to walk in this and do it?"

Seth responded, "Every day, a little bit more. You must train just like you train to put your spirit man forward or to see in the spirit. The Father wants us to walk in excellence, always."

Adina added, "All right. I know a little something about that."

Stephanie asked, "Practicing or the Spirit of Excellence?"

Adina replied, "Maybe both. We have been in churches that would talk about the Spirit of Excellence and wanted to walk in that, but they had so much control and the desire to appear wealthy. That was their definition of the Spirit of Excellence. It wasn't necessarily walking with integrity but was 'everything needs to look beautiful' when you entered the building. To them, that was the Spirit of Excellence.

"That's not it. That's superfluous. It's fluff. It's an image, but it's not the real thing. The real thing is what Seth did that cost him his life on earth.

"You can walk in excellence and live in a humble abode. It isn't being picked up in a limousine and having the world's pleasures; the world's comfort, Excellence, contains true humility. That could be a part of it, hand in hand with it. It's doing the right thing all the time, which is integrity. It's doing something and doing it well, with the motivation being to do it with excellence so that God gets the glory. When you take the glory for yourself, that is not the Spirit of Excellence; that's pride.

"Stephanie, I saw, as you were talking earlier, about the Spirit of Excellence and how it is like a being and it's an image. It's transparent, and we put it on—we step into it; we become one with it.

"It's a different take on having it stand up inside you. You want it inside you, but then you're walking in it. You tell it to stand up, and we stand in it. We step into it and it completely envelopes us, so you don't know the difference between it and us. It's like the goal of the Christian life at the end. Hopefully, we have so much Jesus in us that He is seen, not us. That is excellence.

"Are you doing things with excellence? Not shipwrecking on a bad day, and are you doing it for his glory and not your own? Are you doing your job and doing it well? Or are you cutting corners?

"If Noah had cut corners because it was taking decades and decades more than a human lifetime today, that ship may not have lasted as long as it did. They could have had many issues. He had all the animals in it. He had to figure out how to keep the animals safe. And if they were mating, there were babies. And they had to store the food for a year, not just for themselves, but also for the animals. How did they do the practical stuff? He had to have a lot of wisdom on how to build it according to the plans. If he had cut corners and cheated, it may not have lasted. It might have been a leaky boat, and then everybody would've been in trouble.

"It's the same in our life. We may be tempted to cut corners because we don't have integrity and don't work with excellence—that requires more from us. It takes longer to do it with excellence."

Stephanie added, "It comforts me to know I can step into the entity of Excellence. And that's not in my strength. That makes me happy."

Adina continued, "Yes, I see myself stepping into that being—the Spirit of Excellence, and we became one with it. It is entirely on the inside of me, but also completely covering me.

Stephanie remarked, "It takes the pressure off. If you think of what you said, a key point for me was that the boat took longer to build than even a lifetime we live today. That's huge for people to grasp. And second, when you said if the animals mated, I mean, they had to live in the dung of everything."

Adina added, "Well, that's the practical stuff. How did they handle all the excrement that's coming from these animals? They had to have a system to get it off the boat.

They had to get it out, store it, or dump it so that it didn't bring disease because that's what happens otherwise.

"There's the question. Did the animals continue to mate, or did the Lord stop that process that year, so they didn't go through their normal cycles? Did that happen? We don't know. Those are questions we can discuss when we get to Heaven, but Noah had to build the boat with excellence, and his sons helped him. There were only eight of them total—his wife, their three sons, and their wives, and they were the only ones left on the earth."

Stephanie remarked, "I can't even imagine."

Adina added, "Building with excellence means building it to last. We have the Spirit of Excellence.

Ron added, "Remember, too, Noah was made perfect in his generations, so he had none of the encumbrances from his bloodline, which gave more room for excellence to stand up.

> *Mirror God; you are his offspring. ² This is how: let the love of Christ be your life; remember how he abandoned himself to us. His love is contagious, not reluctant but extravagant. Sacrificial love pleases God like the sweet aroma of worship. ³ Love has nothing in common with lust, immoral acts, or greed. The absence of these motives even in the way you talk sets a **standard of excellence**. ⁴ Any distorted language sarcasm or below the belt jokes are uncalled for much*

rather let gratitude race your conversations. ⁵ The Christ life gives distinct definition to the Kingdom of God. You cannot live a double standard life abusing people through adultery, lust and greed is like worshiping a distorted image of yourself which is what idolatry is all about. (Ephesians 5:1-5) (MIRROR) (Emphasis added)

The definition of a standard is an agreed way of doing something. Paul is speaking of an agreed way of excellence. A standard is also a banner for claiming possession of something.

Step into the Spirit of Excellence today. Let it become one with you and you with him! You are a son who is to live in the Spirit of Excellence.

———·———

Chapter 32
The Kingdom Dynamic of Stepping into Position

Heaven has been teaching us several things recently:

1. To recognize that we are sons.
2. To allow this revelation to revolutionize our way of life.
3. To live spirit forward and not from our soul.
4. To call the Glory of God within us to stand up.
5. To recognize and step into our place as legislative and judicial sons.
6. Begin to rule as a legislative and judicial son.

⁶ For unto us a Child is born, unto us a Son is given; and the government will be upon His shoulder. And His name will be called Wonderful, Counselor, Mighty God, Everlasting Father, Prince of Peace. ⁷ Of the increase of His government and peace there will be no end, upon the throne of David and over His kingdom, to order it and establish it with judgment and justice from that time forward, even forever. The zeal of the Lord of hosts will perform this. (Isaiah 9:6-7)

Our responsibility is to release the government of God in our jurisdiction.

Behold, I give you the authority to trample on serpents and scorpions, and over all the power of the enemy, and nothing shall by any means hurt you. (Luke 10:19)

In the Mirror Bible, it reads,

See, I have given you authority to trample upon serpents and scorpions and every powerful symbolic disguise of the enemy. Nothing shall by any means nullify your authentic identity. Your likeness is secured in me. (Luke 10:19) (MIRROR)

Next Steps:

- Simply do not permit lawlessness in your territories.
- Utilize the angelic forces.
- Commission them to work to release the peace and the Kingdom of God that accompanies the government of God.
- Utilize chaos nets.
- Build the shields.
- Commission them to patrol the gates and bridges.

- Remember, the sons *must know* they are sons in order to son!
- Work with the Watchers and Patrollers in your territories.
- Determine if Consequential Liens are involved.

Dominions on Land

Angels use the brown capture bags to capture land that was taken captive by the enemy. It is essentially "illegal land," or land under an illegal ownership claim. Unlike the domains which can be captured in the Orange Bag, it is different because this one deals with physical earth. In the situation we saw, it was the result of a consequential lien that a principality put upon a region of land or someone's stolen land. This was an encroaching of an evil dominion upon land.

When a consequential lien is placed upon a region of land, it is an encroaching of an evil dominion upon land.

We then saw where natural land had been cursed by the bloodshed that occurred on it, and the land had been stolen. The legal right was two-fold—the shedding of innocent blood and the theft of the land. These gave the legal right to the principality to overlay an evil dominion on someone's territory or land mass in the natural.

Remember the account in the book of Daniel about princes being over regions—like the Prince of Persia being over a region that was an entire land mass. It contained an entire body of people. The freedom from the principality is for individuals' sakes and families' sakes. This pertains to land stolen from people, even in the natural. Think of it as the land that the Native Americans had stolen from them. An evil dominion has been placed over them and their heritage—an evil dominion that can be easily captured and dismantled.

Repentance work that has already been done concerning land that has been taken like that can be applied for the capture bags by simply commissioning the angels to retrieve the land and remove the captured principality. Other repentance work may also be needed. Be led by Holy Spirit in that arena.

The ability to remove the principality is a part of the parameter and will be a useful tool when dealing with parameters seen on someone's life as a trust. The Godly trust in this is all that Heaven has for us, including inheritances stolen from us— including land.

In a vision, we saw an actual natural land mass. We saw a coastline and a castle on a hill overlooking the ocean. We saw the whole land mass captured, then we saw the evil domain overlaying the captured land mass. This brown capture bag, used in conjunction with removing consequential liens, is to capture the dominion and free the land mass. "Is it that easy to capture the dominion?" we asked Malcolm. "Well, yes! This IS Heaven!" he exclaimed.

Instead of dealing with little peon demons, we are dealing with principalities and getting it over with. We are just now beginning to understand the magnitude of the finished work of Jesus with the simplicity of what we have as sons of God because of His finished work and His blood that was shed. This is the work of Heaven and the Kingdom Dynamics.

How does this work concerning cities? There are evil dominions who have taken over land masses and cities. Remember the Prince of Persia. As we are doing this work with the capture bags given to the angels, it is like what was used by the angel that visited Daniel. That is what was used then and will be used now—a brown capture bag.

Imagine individual brown capture bags related to every state of the United States. Imagine looking at each state in the natural and then seeing in the spirit, the overlay of the evil dominion over each state, city, or town. Now see the bloodshed that has occurred over them. That is how the dominion can take authority.

One of the first things to look at concerning the legal right a prince exercises is innocent bloodshed, followed by profane worship and all the things you've been taught related to this. That is why that information was the forerunner of understanding this paradigm now.[23]

Begin Repentance

Begin repentance for the shedding of innocent blood and then for profane worship. Follow Heaven's direction concerning other areas of repentance.

Requests for Your Angels

- *I speak to my soul and instruct you to take a step back.*
- *I call my spirit forward now.*
- *I yield to my spirit this day.*
- *I call the Glory of God within me to stand up.*
- *I step into the realms of Heaven.*
- *I step into my place as a legislative and judicial son.*
- *I step into the Spirit of Excellence.*
- *I call the angels assigned to me to come near.*
- *I request warring angels, backup angels, and others of the Heavenly hosts.*
- *I request for these angels:*
  - *Chaos nets*
  - *Fog dispeller*
  - *Timed devices*
  - *Booby traps*
  - *Bows & Arrows*

---

[23] Taken from *Kingdom Dynamics – Volume 1 & Dealing with Trusts & Consequential Liens in the Courts of Heaven.*

- *Cannons*
- *Capture bags of every size, color and dimension, particularly the brown capture bags for the capturing of evil dominions.*
- *Angel food, bread, and elixir*
- *Other weapons as designated by Heaven.*
- *Maps, keys, and the strategies of Heaven.*

Commissioning

I repent for those in league with the workers of darkness who are seeking to cause chaos, and destruction in my territories. I forgive them, bless them, and release them, in the name of Jesus Christ.

I request the closure of every portal of hell that has been opened by the sacrifice of innocent bloodshed, pagan worship, and ungodly trades by these persons and those in league with them. I request the cancellation of every trade resulting from the innocent bloodshed through abortion and the sacrifice of children and adults in this nation.

I call my angels near, and I request warring angels and back up angels.

I request for you and the other angels of the host, chaos nets, fog dispeller, timed devices, booby traps, bows and arrows, cannons, capture bags of every color, size and dimension, and purpose, angel food, angel bread, angel elixir, and all other weapons as needed and required to do your duty.

I commission you to the full use of every weapon, and strategy, in the name of Jesus to successfully establish and maintain peace in my regions, domains, realms, and territories.

I release the lightning of God into my realms, territories, regions, and domains, in the name of Jesus Christ.

I commission you to capture every domain and dominion that has been set up by hell and its workers. Bring them into subjection to the feet of Jesus.

I release the peace of God over my city, town, village, county, state, and nation, in the name of Jesus, the risen one.

I request from the Court of Cancellations the cancellation of every assignment of hell against those territories under my jurisdiction as a legislative and judicial son.

Declaration

In the name of Jesus Christ, I declare as a legislative and judicial son of God:

That the peace of God shall reign over my realms, territories, landscapes, dimensions, city (or town), county (or parish), state, and nation.

There shall be no upheaval for I govern my jurisdiction by my authority as a son of God.

I say NO to unrest, rioting, destruction, mayhem, and anarchy.

I say NO to "the purge" as that has been released upon my nation.

I say, "It shall NOT be! Not on my watch!" It shall quickly come to naught.

There shall be NO expansion of evil in my territories, but my territories shall become a place of delight in the Glory of God.

I stand in my authority as a son and co-reign with Jesus, the risen one with whom I am also risen.

The government of God shall reign this day and in the coming days over my arche, in Jesus' name.

Chaos and other works of darkness shall be shut down entirely in Jesus' name.

There shall be confusion and chaos in the leadership of the agents of darkness seeking to organize this destruction.

Every assignment of hell coming from any counsel of hell of ANY time shall be immediately cancelled and thrown down and come to naught in time and out of time and in every dimension. The fowler angels shall capture and subdue completely every foul bird, in Jesus' name.

Every evil spirit shall be brought into captivity.

Every demonic plot shall fail and come to nothing.

Peace SHALL reign, the government of God shall reign because I declare it so, in the name of Jesus Christ, the resurrected one.

Now pray boldly in the Spirit!

———·———

Chapter 33
The Kingdom Dynamic of Projected Glory

We asked, "Father, what is your heart?" We said, "Take us where you want us to go, Jesus."

We began walking up a wide stairway made of a pearly substance. Initially, Stephanie wore glass slippers but stepped out of them to walk barefoot on the stairs. With every step she took, the stairs illuminated beneath her feet. Everything above her was a beautiful azure blue. As she stepped onto the final stair, everything in front of her lit up with bright white light—complete illumination.

We learned that our instructor for this day was Adam. He instructed her to move forward. As she did, the sky changed into a beautiful after-sunset sky, what you would see at dusk. As she moved forward, she could almost feel smoke around her. It was smoke from an incense burner. A place on the ground that was round and orange was highlighted to her, so she went to stand on it.

Immediately when she did, she could see Jesus. It felt like she was looking at a hologram. Wondering what this was, she heard the word 'encapsulated.' She sensed that with every move she made, Jesus was making the exact same move. It was a picture of His presence residing within her. If He moved, she moved. It showed what being quantum entangled with Him looks like. His presence, residing in her and in everything she does. She was mirroring Him as if she was encapsulated and entangled with His presence.

She remarked, "What I am realizing is that from where I am standing, about five feet in front of me all the way around, which is what is represented by this orange area on the floor, is the Glory emanating from me because Jesus is here, but I am also encapsulated in this realm.

As she looked deeper, she could see that even below her feet, the Glory stood out about five feet from where she was and above her. It was projecting from her.

Adam said, "It is greater and bigger than an anointing. The word "anointing" has been misused. This is emanating; it is encapsulated. This is projected because it is not in and of yourself."

We asked to be taught about this, and as soon as we asked, we saw a scene like on the television game show "The Price is Right." The game was where a prize was behind one of three doors. A door opened, and she could see people all around, people we knew and people who work with or are associated with the ministry. You could see who had this projection of the Glory. You could see who is walking in it and who is not."

We heard the phrase, **"Deep calls to deep."** Adam said,

---
*When a spirit knows a spirit—
those that are walking in this
and are projecting the Glory
because of Jesus will recognize others
who are doing the same.*

We recognized that we, as humans, could slide over into judging others easily. We wanted our hearts to remain pure in this matter. We asked, "Will you give clarity and wisdom and understanding from Heaven about this?"

The instruction was to walk, so Stephanie began walking. As she walked, she noticed a light surrounding her. It wasn't the deep orange she had seen before, but it was like a bubble of light in front of her. It was the essence—the projected Glory in front of her. As she walked, she could see people coming from all different directions. As people crossed her path, some recognized the essence with her. They also had the same essence with them. It was a knowing in the spirit. It was as if the person with it turns and recognizes it in her, and she could recognize it in them. She could see a light and a flame within those who were not projecting the Glory. It was the potential for the projected Glory.

Adam explained, "As you see those with the lit flame inside but have not yet walked into this positioning, know that Heaven is working to bring them to the place of projecting the Glory. She suddenly saw the people walking around with the lit flame inside them stop. They turned and gathered around each person that was projecting the Glory. They were drawn to them. They were drawn to Jesus who is within each person emanating the Glory."

She asked, "What do you want us to know about this?"

She was taken back to when she first walked up the stairs and how every step she took was illuminated under her feet. She remembered removing the slippers, and Adam said, "This is about intimacy." As she ascended the stairs, each step was lit before her.

This is about intimacy.

Stephanie inquired, "Is the understanding we are supposed to have about intimacy?"

"Much more," she was told. "It begins with intimacy. You begin climbing the stairs with intimacy. "

> *Paths are illuminated*
> *as you understand the reality*
> *that Jesus is in you,*
> *and you are in Him.*

"Then, as you walk about in the world, people are being drawn to you. You can also recognize those with a similar spirit. You are about to take the next steps."

The Next Steps

Adam said, "See the angels around each person with that projected Glory and the people drawn to them. Signs and wonders are happening. Binding and loosing occur along with regeneration in the body."

We noted that Adam looked different than he had at other times when we saw him. His skin appeared translucent. Stephanie could see everything inside him—every bone, ligament, and his heart. Adam said, "This is what I looked like in the garden before the fall."

Adam began writing on a whiteboard, and Stephanie soon began to read this new information.

The first word she saw was "structure." Underneath that word was the word "parallel." Under that word was "diagrams." The next word was "theorem." Underneath that was the word "case-by-case." Underneath that was the word "idiosyncrasies" and underneath that was the word "ease."

Adam explained, "What you have seen and walked in is an evidence-based theorem. Yes, you will see these things with your physical and your spiritual eyes."

What we had seen was the projected Glory in front of us and around us and realized it was Jesus, but others were being drawn to it.

Adam continued, "This picture is about walking intimately with Jesus and the Father—walking carefully.

"The projected five-foot barrier is indeed the Glory, but it is a barrier of protection against the mindset of pride. When you have the reality of knowing that Jesus, who is much taller, is standing behind you and that you are in this place with Him, enveloped, encapsulated, and projecting His Glory, it is Him that people are drawn to and not the person that has this. Therefore, it feels impossible to walk pridefully because that person clearly understands the theorem."

Stephanie interjected, "I now hear the word 'idiosyncrasies.'" An idiosyncrasy is an odd habit or a quirk. But Heaven defines it as an individualizing characteristic."

As we walk in this, it is the idiosyncrasies of Jesus they will be drawn to—his individual characteristics. Not you. It is a fail-safe—a Kingdom principle."

She then asked, "What are parallels?"

She immediately saw a picture of paralleling what Jesus does. We will parallel Him. "Mimic" is not the right word, but it is the way we can do what He does—what He did while here on earth and when he walked in Heaven—He was in both places all the time.

Stephanie asked, "How am I supposed to walk it out?"

The entity—Deep

Ron interjected, "Adina was informed the other night that deep is an entity. Deep calls to deep."

Stephanie asked, "Is this an entity we are in?"

Adam responded, "Indeed, just like the Spirit of Excellence is an entity, Deep is an entity."

What we were learning felt like layers we had been stepping into. We have learned to call our spirit forward; we ask Glory to rise within us, step into our sonship, then we step into the Spirit of Excellence and embolden ourselves.

Adam was saying that we had to come to the understanding, relevance, and revelation that as we have taken off the old garments, we are stepping into the new—layer upon layer.

To recognize others who are projecting Glory, realize it is a deep calling unto deep.

We asked, "How do you want us to learn how to notice the things that are working in each individual?"

Adam replied, "Disharmony is an entity, but so is Harmony." He leaned in and asked, what would you do with that information if you had it?" Meaning, if we knew who was not walking in Harmony versus who was?

We responded, "That is a good question, Adam. I will leave it to you to answer that for us, please."

He said, "The question should be, what should you do?"

We asked, "What should we do, Adam?"

He replied, "Well, what is the opposite of disharmony?"

"Harmony," we said.

He instructed us, "Talk to the intercessors about constantly releasing bonds, but not just bonds, entities. Step into the entities."

We asked him to write the bonds/entities to request on the board. He began,

- "Bond of Sure-footedness.
- Bond of Excellence.
- Bond of Calling for the Deep.
- Bond of the Revelation of the Entity of Excellence, the Entity of Deep, and the Entity that is Revelation.
- The Bond of Stepping In and Stepping Upon.
- The Bond of Unity brings Harmony.

Release these upon the people."

In immediate response to his instruction, we began...

We ask to step into the Court of Titles and Deeds through Jesus, Your Honor.

We request for everyone and their families that work for or are employed or contracted with or draw near to LifeSpring International Ministries, the Bond of Emboldened, Sure-footedness, Excellence, Calling for the Deep, Revelation of the Entity of Excellence, and of the entity that is Deep, and the Entity that is Revelation, Stepping In and Stepping Upon, and the Bond of Unity that brings Harmony, in Jesus' name.

We ask that these be released to each realm, to be recorded upon each book, this day, in the name of Jesus. We ask that the angels assigned to us draw near. We commission you to bring to each of us these bonds, to rest it upon us, to co-labor with the angels assigned to LifeSpring and the Bond Registry Angels, and to bring all of this to light.

We ask that you teach us to step into Emboldened, Sure-footedness, Excellence, the entity that is Deep, that is Revelation, that is Stepping In and Stepping Upon, and that is Unity that brings Harmony.

Father, we thank you for the entities you created for your sons. That way, we may rest in this, that we are encapsulated by your Glory. That this projects out, and people are drawn to it because it is Jesus. May we be excellent in this Father. Thank you for the understanding and revelation that you are giving us—that you are pouring out, in Jesus' name.

———·———

Chapter 34

The Kingdom Dynamic of a Turning Tide

Stephanie and I stepped into Heaven hearing shouts of "glory," "honor," and "worthy." We were taken to a high cliff overlooking an ocean. We weren't drawn to the ocean, only to the sound. We could hear the waves lapping in and out. Then we heard, "The tide is turning." The song, "I Know My Redeemer Lives" began playing with these lyrics: "Who taught the sun where to stand in orbit, who told the ocean you can only come this far?"

She then heard the Lord Jesus speak, "I beckon the waves to come to and fro. I can turn the tide. The ocean flows at my beckoning. I can turn them any way I want." Suddenly, it felt like a Job moment. "If I can do that, who are you going to believe? The well-laid plans of the Lord are your strength. With that in mind, who are you going to trust? You? Others who speak about you? Or the one who beckons the waves, and who tells the ocean it can only come this far.

"Will you walk in your sonship in understanding, trusting the one who can beckon the tide? Or are you going to trust in someone else and what they say? There are already a lot of voices. More are coming. A lot of voices—who will you hear? Are you going to listen to the silence of the sound? Or are will you hear the roar of His voice and trust it?"

David added, "When we stepped in, I saw a hall of mirrors, and so I asked, 'Why am I seeing this?' I heard, 'It is to reveal the reflection of God's image—your true identity.'"

When the Lord was just speaking and He said the word, "sonship," that was confirming. It's important to point out that the mirror is a reflection. When you look in the mirror, what reflection do you see? What is the thing that you observe? I relate it to the first 23 years of my life; when I looked in the mirror, I didn't see David because of my identity issues.

Stephanie remarked, "David, you heard the enemy's voice instead of the one that wanted to speak to you about your sonship. Who were you going to believe?"

David replied, "Yes, so now I see myself as God sees me. I've learned how to do that. I've learned how to embrace it. I've learned how to accept it. The message to me is clear about our sonship, but whose voice will you listen to in the process of learning about your sonship?—the one that beckons the ocean and tells it where it stops, or the one that lies to you?"

David continued, "What you hear, you process. How much energy or thought are you going to give to it? Scripture says, 'As a man thinks, in his heart, so he is.' That's true. Who are you going to listen to? It seems important that the identity of the sonship is solidified.

"This morning, I got up, and one of the first things that came to mind was governmental, legislative, and jurisdictional sons. I began to talk to the Father, and I said, 'Father, give me revelation of this. I know it won't happen overnight, but I know this is what you have. I asked for Heaven's directive to lead me and process this into me, process me so that I will become the very thing that was spoken.'"

Adina remarked, "Yes. In John 10, Jesus said that 'my sheep hear my voice, and they follow.' We are all sheep, but I think there's a progression. There is the *teknon*[24] son, and then there's the *uihos*[25] son where you can be about your Father's business. You have his trust, instruction, and confidence that you will do business his way, right? That's what the son could do. The *uihos* son could conduct business as though he were the father. He had the father's business and the father's best interest and not his own agenda—that's a *uihos* son. If you have your own agenda, you're not a *uihos* son. And there are a lot of those in the pulpits and in church leadership with their own agendas. That doesn't make you a son who can

---

[24] Teknon – a small child.
[25] Uihos – pronounced "wee-os"

legislate—acting in the Father's interest and being trusted as a son. You can't trust everyone.

"It matters who you listen to. Proverbs says, 'life and death are in the power of the tongue.' There is authority and creative or destructive power in words. We all know that. What you hear, including what you are rehearsing in your mind, is either life-giving or life-taking. It's creating the Kingdom of God or it's bringing destruction to you.

"There is a whole lot in the voice and the sound. Not just the frequency of the sound. I haven't studied frequency so, I know very, very little about it. I don't understand a whole lot about it as far as spiritual matters go, but the sound itself and what it carries and the Father's voice. When you speak as He is speaking, that's different than when just Adina is speaking. When He is speaking through you, when His voice is coming through your voice. It carries such weight and creative power that regular words don't carry. There are many layers of understanding the power of the Father speaking through us and how our words create.

"Understanding these concepts will help us grow and not just be sheep. Sheep are herded and nurtured. They are like babies. Sheep are like the *'teknon'* son."

Adina continued, "Sheep wander. They must be corralled all the time. They have to be watched and practically spoon-fed. I see them as baby Christians who can't be trusted with the Father's business. The Father can't put them in a position to extend His Kingdom when they must be corralled. They either have to be behind a fence or be trained to listen to his voice. Does that make sense? Am I making sense?"

———·———

Chapter 35
The Kingdom Dynamic of the Wellspring of Life

Stephanie began, "I don't know why I'm always in a garden, but that's where we are again. I'm on a very distinct path of a garden. I guess it's because Heaven has gardens everywhere.

"This is outside of our LifeSpring complex. I've come to a spring, and I heard the phrase 'wellspring of life.' May I ask who's talking to me because I hear you talking. It feels like Malcolm.

"Malcolm, can you come into view for me?" Malcolm said, "Where is the Wellspring of Life?"

Stephanie replied, "I don't know where the Wellspring of Life is." Malcolm then showed Stephanie that this spring is inside of her. He instructed, "Draw from it."

Stephanie responded, "Okay, I will draw from this Wellspring of Life inside me."

Malcolm said, "Doesn't it seem refreshing?"

She replied, "It does, Malcolm. When you initially asked me that question, I figured it was inside of me, but I was going to hear your answer." He just showed me a very clear picture of a Christian who doesn't understand drawing from the Wellspring of Life in them, and they don't realize just how dry they are.

Stephanie asked, "Malcolm is this their soul or their spirit?"

"It's their spirit," he said. Malcolm asked, "What has the church age brought to the people?"

Stephanie replied, "My first thought is confusion."

He said, "That is a correct answer. How does one know where to tap in?"

She responded, "I'm going to say through correct teaching. Am I right, Malcolm? Because I don't know where this is going, and it feels like the basics to me. You have been talking about keeping it simple. Many are getting caught up in confusion."

Malcolm asked, "What does Father want more than anything?" Stephanie replied, "He wants a relationship, doesn't he?"

He replied, "That is the Wellspring of Life. Remind people to step in, to be with Him. These spiritual encounters are necessary, but the relationship is vital. A lot of revelation knowledge is coming and has been given. I am reminding you of the relational aspect of the

Wellspring of Life. The vital nature for the spirit is the relational aspect of stepping in and drawing from the Wellspring of Life—which is Jesus.

"This *is* going back to the basics, isn't it?" Stephanie asked.

Malcolm responded, "Yes, and as you go back to the basics and draw from the wellspring, the rest of the knowledge, the quantum, the stars—all of that, the soul will be able to handle better because of the relationship."

"How will the people govern without the relational aspect of the wellspring of life? Think of these times, these moments as checkpoints. Think of these times, these moments of receiving heavenly revelation as checkpoints."

He then showed a picture of someone driving and coming to a checkpoint. He said, "You must have a pass to proceed through the checkpoint. Without it, you can't go further or deeper. People need to be reminded of that.

"You see, you are dealing with many people who are new to working in the heavenly realms as sons.[26] They are catching on and gaining quickly, but they must get out their pass and show it to go further. The pass is what they will show at the checkpoint."

---

[26] Gyroscopes assist in stability and guidance systems.

Stephanie replied, "Well, I am getting out my pass." Malcolm took it, stamped it, handed it back to her, and laughed. "Thank you, Malcolm."

Ezekiel's Gyroscope

As Malcolm ended his instruction, we summoned Ezekiel. He appeared wearing a crown and held a gyroscope in his hand. He was standing in front of a giant gyroscope awaiting a commission.

Stephanie explained, "Ron, he needs two things from the Father.

"Father, we request for Ezekiel, his commanders, and ranks gyroscopes and a large gyroscope."

We received the items and then commissioned Ezekiel to the full use of them for the Glory of the King. We then were instructed to commission them to release these items into the realms of all who are a part of LifeSpring.

Stephanie then asked Ezekiel, "Why do you wear a crown?"

He replied, "It's a picture of you as sons. It's a reminder of what you wear." Stephanie asked, "Are we to request crowns?"

Ezekiel responded, "I have crowns for the sons from the Father. Part of your governing is to commission me to bestow on the sons the gift of the crowns."

Stephanie remarked, "It feels like these crowns are connected to this place that is the giant gyroscope. It's an entry point we come through as sons as we learn about quantum and paradigms. He just showed me a bag full of crowns from the Father. What a gift!

Ezekiel, we commission you to deliver the crowns to the sons as deemed by Heaven according to their scrolls."

He then walked inside the giant gyroscope and disappeared immediately.

Lydia's Encouragement

As Ezekiel left, Lydia appeared.

Stephanie noted that the giant gyroscope seemed to be in a positional place near the LifeSpring complex.

Lydia said, "Many will come through this place. This is a permission to the Body to walk through this place in Heaven. This is specific to LifeSpring."

Stephanie immediately thought of the television show Quantum Leap. She said, "This is part of their discovery."

Lydia said, "Some will see the gyroscope, and some will hear the frequency of it. Some will know that they are standing in it, and some will feel the presence of it around them as they learn to come to this place."

Lydia then showed us how eyes, ears, thoughts, and feelings would be opened as they walk through the knowing of this quantum.

Stephanie remarked, "It feels like the next level. It feels like this is what's coming. This is next. And since we've already walked in quantum, this will be new. Thank you, Lydia."

———·———

Chapter 36

The Kingdom Dynamic of the Need to Govern Voices

Engaging with Heaven, we walked on pavers toward a gazebo on a hill. Someone was sitting at the gazebo posed like Auguste Rodin's statue *The Thinker*.

We turned around, and Malcolm was standing with us, eating an apple. He asked, "What do you think Adam was thinking right before he bit into the fruit?"

We hadn't thought of an answer to his question, so we waited for what he'd say next. He said, "Wouldn't you say this is a silhouette of the picture of Adam? This was the rest of his life," he said, nodding to the statue. "That moment was forever imprinted on his mind. He thought about it day in and day out. What would have been different? What could have been? After he ate, the rest of his life was full of would-haves and should-haves. But what was he thinking about before he tasted?"

I felt compelled to go over and put my hand on the right shoulder of this statue.

Stephanie asked, "What is an inflection?"

Merriam-Webster's Dictionary has multiple definitions for the word *inflection*. One of those definitions is the act or result of curving or bending. We sensed that Heaven was highlighting the word "bend" to us.

Stephanie asked, "Are you showing me that there was a bend towards something?" As she walked around the statue, she noted the picnic tables nearby, the apple, the garden, and the statue as a representation frozen in time. Malcolm noted, "Adam's thoughts of that day were frozen forever in time in his mind. It was a constant image before him and an absolute accusation against him his entire life."

Wondering what we needed to learn about this, she heard two words: *fall* (like the fall of man) and *sovereignty*.

Now the statue became Adam, so we greeted him. She continued, "Hi, Adam. I keep hearing the word inflection which means to bend. Can you tell me more?"

Adam, in turn, asked, "Have you considered the bend in my heart and mind that caused me to take the apple? Consider it. I wouldn't have taken it without a bend."

We had never thought of it like that, where something was already going on with him. Whether it was idolizing his wife, thoughts in his mind, or something else.

Stephanie asked him, "Would there have been? How could there have been anything? You walked with the Father in the cool of the day? What made you take the apple?"

He said, "Therein lies the bend."

She replied, "Well, Adam, I do not pretend to know your heart in the moment, so you will have to tell us. The only thing I could think of was that whispers had already been spoken to cause mistrust or to cause you to put all your eggs in that basket that was Eve."

Again, he said, "Therein lies the bend. Sin lied with me, not with her." (And 'lied' became multiple meanings).

"Why would he eat the fruit?" Stephanie asked.

I replied, "He got into his soul."

We surmised that even though the fall had not yet happened, Adam had a free will. He had been hearing whispers (from the accuser, who later took the form of a serpent), and these whispers became accusations. Because the Father had created Adam with free will, the Father was going to ensure that Adam could choose regardless of the outcome of that choice.

When he was not walking with Jesus or the Father in the cool of the day, there were whispers he was hearing. It may not have created doubt as we think of doubt now, but these whispers were things he thought about, which created the bend. And there had been enough pondering and bending that when presented with the opportunity, he acted on it.

Wanting confirmation that we understood correctly, we asked, "Are we right, Adam?"

He replied, "Therein lies the bend."

Stephanie noted that as he said that he was pointing to Eve, who came from him—from inside of him.

He showed how Eve could step into him because she came out of him spiritually. She was like a perfect smaller version of him with long hair. She was a piece of him and came from him. Therein lies the bend: she ate.

Adam said, "Upon this earth, Eve was all I knew in the physical and therein lies the bend."

We asked, "Adam, is it because of your free will in that moment? Were the whispers about losing her or maybe fear? What was it?"

He said, "The whispers were about not governing my territory. I did not have to accept the whispers, nor did I have to allow them. If you have ever seen movies before where someone is walking around, and they hear an audible whisper, and the sound is all around them. That is what it was like. I would just be walking, and I would hear something."

This all had to do with the word inflection because Satan would take the word and bend it. Adam didn't govern to remove that action. Satan would take a word and change it. He placed an inflection upon it. An inflection modifies the original word, it bends it and changes the meaning.

We asked, "What do we take from this?"

We again saw the silhouette of The Thinker, but it was not Adam, as he was standing with us beside Malcolm.

Your soul will think you into destructive action.

Adam said, "I spent the rest of my life thinking about the would-haves and the should-haves, and it was a burden."

Suddenly, Adam's first two sons Cain and Abel walked up next to him, and Adam said, "The would-have and the should-have," which is how he introduced them.

Malcolm said, "This message is about the value of living spirit-forward where there is no inflection or bend except towards the Father's heart. Choose this day whom you will serve."

When you live spirit-forward,
it is much easier to serve the Father
and to stay out of the thinking
of the soul.

It says in the Word that our thoughts would be higher—our thoughts are higher."[27]

---

[27] Isaiah 55:8-9

Malcolm said, "That is spirit-talk right there."

We closed the engagement, thanking them for helping us, and then the statue of "The Thinker" stood and walked away.

———·———

Chapter 37
The Kingdom Dynamic
of Timing Devices

Heaven taught us about an angelic weapon called *Timed Devices* a few years ago. We discussed this in the book, *Engaging Heaven for Revelation – Volume 1*.[28]

In this engagement with Heaven, we learned about a very different item known as *Timing Devices*. Stephanie and I had been discussing the concept of cycles of time and how some people experience attacks in certain areas of their life at the same time each year or each month repetitively. You may notice a particular month of the year you're apprehensive about. You recognize cycles of misfortune or calamity that seem to come during that

---

[28] *Engaging Heaven for Revelation – Volume 1,* LifeSpring Publishing (2020).

time. With that on our minds, Heaven began to unpack how to deal with this situation in the Courts of Heaven.

Timing devices are encroachments upon our timeline designed like a bomb to go off at pre-appointed times. When we asked if we could get more insight, Moses joined us and said the word 'frequencies.'

We watched as the ground opened before us to a picture of what hell would be. The frequencies from hell are oracles.[29] Our instruction from Moses to deal with these frequencies was to shorten them so they could not reach us.

We paused, and two phrases came to mind: *chain of events* and *deciphering of the timelines*. We understood that these were hell's strategies. Hell is deciphering timelines. Hell uses people in conjunction with lingering human spirits on assignment to create hell on earth for many people. We need to repent on behalf of those human agents being used.

Cycle of Events.

The understanding of a cycle of events has to do with generational things. Helping people deal with their generational line and bringing repentance for the issues we find is critical work. We also need to look down on the generational timeline where these Timing Devices

---

[29] An oracle is an authoritative opinion or decision.

are put in place. The chain of events in this cycle is like chains of bondage and taxation.

How do we do that?

First, identify the problem. Find the first inception of this form of taxation being placed on the family line. Do not be fooled. Individuals can put this upon themselves when they walk in the works of darkness. This can be generational and regular sin. We need to include both ourselves and our families in our prayer paradigm. Wisdom is key here. Wisdom will unlock the eyes of our understanding as we search for, hear, and see the storyline.

Once you have identified the problem then ask when taxation was placed on the family line. Then, offer repentance. Finally, request the shortening of the frequencies.

Court of Covenant

Moses is taking me on a journey right now. We are looking at the ark amid torrential rains and flooding. He asked, "Would you say this is a time and a season?"

Stephanie said, "I am going to say no."

He said, "Would you say it affected the times and the seasons?"

Stephanie replied, "It did. This will bring newness of life." She asked, "Can you show me which court we will go to for repentance and dismantling this impact upon the times and seasons?"

We were led to a new court—the Court of Covenant. In this court, you could see cubby holes with scrolls everywhere. Moses picked up a scroll and said, "This is the covenant between you and Heaven. This paperwork of our covenant with Father is profound and it enriches understanding.

We can come here and determine if timing devices are placed on our timeline. They are an encroachment of hell because our covenant is with the Father and Heaven. There will be many blows inflicted upon the enemy because of these encroachments. We have permission to come to this Court of Covenant, but this is not so much a court as a records room. The Court of Covenant is separate from the Court of Records.

There are many encroachments here, and we saw an attachment on the back of the scrolls—like an addendum on the back where there have been encroachments.

Sometimes the encroachments are a visceral attack because it has so much momentum. However, the Father will deliver as many blows as necessary to the enemy until they are taken care of. The enemy will receive the blows as soon as they are identified and dismantled.

You obtain legal paperwork from the Court of Covenant and do repentance work on behalf of the generations that set this timing device. This paperwork details the encroachments—the Timing Devices that have been put in place against our timeline and the repentance for the sin(s) that started the process.

We were taught about timed devices that are a weapon that our angels can use on our behalf, but they are different from these Timing Devices of the enemy. The enemy always steals. His motto seems to be, "Why create when I can copy?"

Small Claims Court

Once we have the paperwork from the Court of Covenant due to the repentance for the sins and iniquities of the generations, we take it to the Small Claims Court. This court is entirely different from what we would (in America) consider a small claims court.

This court gets its name because of the *justification of the Father's claim upon us.* It is not like the small claims courts we see on earth. This one in Heaven is much higher.

Stephanie's Story

Stephanie asked, "May we see a court case?"

Moses asked, "Would you like to see yours?"

"Yes," she replied, not realizing it would be about her. She explained, "My children's father died in September." Stephanie had been married when she was young, and the marriage ended in divorce. One year after their separation (in September), he died. His mother and sister, in their grief, blamed Stephanie for his death. They were angry because they had to pick up the pieces of his life after the divorce.

Stephanie continued, "First, I only saw one September, which was his death, but it was two—it was when I left him and when he died. The enemy took that situation because I walked away from the marriage vows, and he used it against me even though the Lord had released me from them."

Stephanie realized Moses was with us because he gave us the law around divorce. Although she had every legal right to divorce him, she wondered what justification the enemy had.

Moses explained, "Because it was under the law."

For clarification, Stephanie asked, "Are you telling me the enemy was able to use the law against me?"

Moses said, "He binds people with the law. There are a lot of people that are under the law. You were under the law of religion then, which he used.

"Because you were entangled with the spirit of religion, that was the entry point. When you detangled yourself from the spirit of religion, this was still present because you had not dismantled it."

"This is an enemy tactic. This strategy is just one way the enemy puts things on people's timelines. Sexual immorality is used as another tactic. By the very act of that immorality, timing devices can be put upon the people. This revelation is an unveiling of those things for your freedom."

We asked, "What else is used besides divorce and sexual immorality?"

Moses said, "Often, it is a matter of looking to see if there is an encroachment. You get to come to the Court of Covenant and find out if there is an encroachment upon your timeline. You invoke Wisdom, look at the storyline, find the original sin, and repent. Then go to the Small Claims Court. This is where the fun begins."

He said, "Do you believe this, Stephanie?"

She replied, "You know that I do. Why did you ask me that?"

He said, "Because seeing is believing that what we see is in the spirit and the natural."

She asked, "Are you saying the freedom of this will be seen in the natural?"

"Let's try it," he said.

We went with him to the Court of Covenant.

I would like to access the Court of Covenant, please.

I would like to see my covenant paperwork with Heaven and the Father.

I call for Wisdom and Council.

The court attendants went over and pulled several scrolls out. They rolled one of them out on the table. There were three encroachments on Stephanie's timeline.

We began repentance for the sins that allowed the placement of these encroachments upon Stephanie's timeline. Once that was completed, we received paperwork from the Court of Covenant to take to the Small Claims Court.

I ask to enter the Small Claims Court.

I call for Wisdom and Council.

I present my paperwork from the Court of Covenant, which details some encroachments upon my timeline, Your Honor.

When we do this, we do not agree with the accuser as we do with accusations because this is an encroachment upon our covenant. **We are acknowledging the encroachment.**[30]

Moses asked, "What is your repentance here?"

She replied, "My appearance today is around obedience, not obedience because I left him, but my disobedience because I married him. I had no business doing that and I did not listen to You."

---

[30] An encroachment is the enemy trying to take what is not his to take.

Moses said, "This is not about the fact that you married somebody. That is not what this is. Marrying him took you both off your timelines."

Stephanie responded, "Well, the Father blessed me with two children. Right? And it set up this taxation in my life, and now that I am looking at it, I was blaming my current husband for this September thing, but it was me. Forgive me for my disobedience. I repent for not listening, which set up this destruction upon my timelines."

Stephanie said, "I see the enemy; he is seething right now.

"I am curious, Your Honor; you said it is not about the fact that I married him. It is about 'obedience is better than sacrifice.' There were a lot of times I was disobedient. The enemy knew what was going on in my first husband's life. I did not.

Chain of Events

"This is where the cycle and chain of events came in because when I disobeyed, it created a chain of events in my life.

"Your Honor, about all the times I was disobedient, did it set up a time cycle of taxation?

"I have repented for my disobedience, and I am now in good standing."

The court attendants brought in three separate Timing Devices. They appeared like small square boxes with a light on the top. The light is illuminated or turned off as if it were armed or disarmed. Each box had chains around it. If the light is off, it means the necessary repentance work has been done to stop its occurrence."

They placed the Timing Devices on a table before her and her attention was drawn to the first one.

Stephanie continued, "I want my timelines returned back into covenant with you. I claim that my life is in covenant with you and that I am forgiven."

The red light turned off and was no longer on.

She was then drawn to the second box. She didn't yet know what this one was concerning.

The Judge looked at the second and third encroachments on her scroll of covenant. The second one was around sexual immorality, but the light on the box was off because of her repentance work. This was in place due to her past sins, and not generational ones.

She asked, "Your Honor, are you saying that this timing device was already deactivated because of repentance?"

The Judge said, "You repented for the curse of the bastard. You did all that, so yes, it is off. The enemy thought he had this in his back pocket to use on you later, but it has been deactivated, and now the Judge is making a public display of the enemy."

The third Timing Device was activated and the light was turned on. It was related to generational iniquities.

Stephanie pleaded, "Your Honor, I have done so much generational work, but it is continual. Will you show me what I can claim here in this court on behalf of my generations to stop this chain of events?

She began to see her mother's face as a young woman in her twenties. Stephanie's mother had specific plans for specific things she thought Stephanie should become. It was a form of control, and it was multi-dimensional. It was not just her, but it was down the family line too. Control was a huge factor in this generational bondage.

"What is the repentance work around the generations?" Stephanie asked.

Your Honor, on behalf of my generations, I repent for the control—for using it and yielding to it.

Father, I repent on their behalf and mine. I asked the blood of Jesus to be applied. I forgive, bless, and release all of them.

I claim that I am in covenant with the one who does control everything.

I want to claim that my times and seasons no longer have these constraints.

In every timeline, I claim victory because of my covenant. May these Timing Devices be used against the enemy and placed on his life.

I claim this from this court because of the encroachment the enemy receives from Heaven, because he encroached upon my covenant.

I request the redemption of every September and the redemption of all other times I have not put my finger on yet.

I request redemption from the Timing Device that has been deactivated.

I claim the full redemption of my times and seasons.

As she prayed, the light went off on the third device. She then asked for the angels to take the timing devices and completely dismantle and destroy them.

Claim Tickets

She then saw three claim tickets in front of her where the timing devices once sat. She picked them up and was directed to the Redemption Center. It was about a covenant renewal—a renewal of the original design.

The Redemption Center

Stephanie declared, "Thank you, your Honor. Thank you for the claims that you have upon my life. Thank you for the covenant. I see my scrolls with the encroachments that are removed from my covenant scrolls and are placed back into the Court of Covenant."

We will discuss the Redemption Center in more depth in a few moments, but first let's talk about a couple of ways we experience loss.

———·———

Chapter 38
The Kingdom Dynamic of Freedom from Taxation & Slavery

What we discussed in the previous chapter pertained to taxations upon our lives. Still, the Redemption Center covers more than just the things lost due to taxation, but also those things lost to trespass and thievery. At times the enemy has trespassed on our territories and stolen things that were not his to steal.

Thievery is periodic.

When we realize the thievery, we can petition the Courts of Heaven either here or in the Court of Reclamation for the restoration of that which has been stolen from us. We also have the caveat that we can request a seven-fold return on things stolen from us by thievery. We have a promise related to this in Proverbs 6:30-31:

> *People do not despise a thief if he steals to satisfy himself when he is starving. ³¹ Yet when he is found, he must restore sevenfold; he may have to give up all the substance of his house.*

We know our enemy is not starving, but he is a thief. We know from John 10:10 the job description of the thief:

> *A thief has only one thing in mind—he wants to steal, slaughter, and destroy. But I (Jesus) have come to give you everything in abundance, more than you expect—life in its fullness until you overflow! (TPT)*

Provision has been made for us:

> *Everything we could ever need for life and complete devotion to God has already been deposited in us by his divine power. For all this was lavished upon us through the rich experience of knowing him who has called us by name and invited us to come to him through a glorious manifestation of his goodness. (2 Peter 1:3) (TPT)*

However, if we do not realize our enemy is a thief and he and his minions want to steal from your life to harm the Father through you, he will have *carte blanche* in your life to steal and ravage your life. In this case, ignorance is NOT bliss—it is unnecessary.

Taxation

The other means of loss comes through taxation. Taxation occurs on a regular basis.

Taxation is systematic.

It may be annually, at a particular time, monthly, or during significant events in one's life. It does not always entail stolen money. It could be the loss of property, children, or others close to you emotionally. Most often, taxation is the result of oaths taken or covenants made by our ancestors, in which case the pathway to freedom is to repent for the profane worship and the ungodly trades that were made in which taxation was promised to the deity of future income or increase. Sometimes the taxation includes the death of someone meeting the criteria for the taxation.

National Taxations

We have found that certain nations always tax those born in that nation. Invariably we find that they have been experiencing taxation upon their lives for as long as they can remember. We have specifically seen it with Haitians, Nigerians, Jamaicans and other nationalities. Due to the dedications of the children born in those nations, the entity (for instance) Nigeria, places a tax on the income and earnings of that child throughout its life. The only thing that stops it is repentance for the dedications and having the claims upon the livelihood dissolved in the Court of Titles and Deeds and Court of Cancellations. You want a transfer of ownership from the entity of the nation to the Lord of Hosts. Remember...

You do not have to be living in one of those nations to experience taxation.

Sometimes the ownership claims are based on the blood shed during childbirth, and the national entity lays claim upon the person because of the shedding of blood.

Remember, blood is a currency in the realm of the spirit.

Realize the nations have a reason for referring to you as subjects. You are subject to their rules, expectations, taxations, and more. You may not have been born in a particular nation to experience taxation. You can be an ancestor of someone born in that nation, and the entity of that nation imposes taxation on the one born in that nation and upon *all* future generations. Parents, you want to get that broken off your children in the Courts of Heaven.

Hidden Nuptials

It is not uncommon to find along with ownership claims upon a person that they have often been married to that national entity. Often they consider the person their personal property through marriage. Usually, the person knows nothing of this marriage arrangement so the pathway to freedom is requesting access to the Divorce Court and asking to see the Registry of Nuptials. In that registry will be a listing of every nuptial to which the person is enjoined. Request an absolute divorce from the national entity. Remove the wedding ring, the veil, and the gown and hand them to the angel for destruction. Then, request the removal of all taxation related to this marriage covenant.

Visiting a Taxing Nation

You don't even have to have been born in a taxing nation or be a descendant of one born to it. You can simply have set foot on the soil of a taxing nation, and they will lay claim on you and your income. You want to be sure to cancel EVERY covenant and EVERY covenant within contract invoked by your presence on that land. Do so in the Court of Cancellations.

> *Father, I request access to the Court of Cancellations.*

> *I repent for coming into agreement for taxation by this taxing national entity, whether knowingly or unknowingly, in Jesus' name. I repent for every ungodly trade made while visiting the taxing nation and while on that nation's soil. I ask you for forgiveness.*

> *I also forgive those who imposed any taxation upon me regarding this, in Jesus' name.*

I am requesting the cancellation of any and all covenants and covenants hidden within contracts that I may have intentionally or unintentionally come into agreement with by my presence in any nation I have visited.

I request the cancellation of every ungodly trade made upon that land, or in preparation to visit that nation. I request the cancellation of every ownership claim made by the entity of that nation upon me and my generations.

Once the repentance is complete and the forgiveness rendered, we can request release from the taxation we have experienced and request restoration of that which has been lost. We will talk about that shortly.

Await the verdict, then request access to the Court of Reclamation. In the Court of Reclamation, request to know of the court what you can request specifically. You may need to visit this court successively over a period of time as this court does not release all you have lost to you all at once. This court releases things stolen gradually.

Dedications of Money

Another avenue for the taxations can be based on dedications we or our ancestors may have made of the monies that come into their hands. The result is described in Haggai 1:6:

You have sown much, and bring in little; you eat, but do not have enough; you drink, but you are not filled with drink; you clothe yourselves, but no one is warm; and he who earns wages, earns wages to put into a bag with holes.

When someone makes a dedication of this sort, they seek to usurp the legal ownership of the money that comes into their hands. Haggai 2:8 reads:

The silver is Mine, and the gold is Mine,' says the LORD of hosts.

The money is simply a medium of exchange.

It is not the property of any one person. It is the property of the Lord of Hosts.

Again, the pathway to freedom is repentance—repentance for the vows made and oaths taken to dedicate all the money that comes into their hand to some false god. Ask for a voiding of the false deed over the money.

This kind of oath was often made to be perpetual—meaning it went from one generation to the next, usually without an end date. You should also request a cancellation of every trade and every benefit of that trade and request a sanctifying of the money that comes into your hands from that time forth, including the money under your stewardship presently.

I request access to the Court of Titles and Deeds.

I am requesting the cancellation of any and all ownership claims by any false gods to the monies that may come into my hands. This money belongs to the Lord of Hosts, according to Haggai 2:8.

I repent for every vow, oath, or covenant undertaken or entered, including any covenants or covenants hidden within contracts that I or my ancestors, or any authority over us at any time may have intentionally or unintentionally come into agreement with.

I request the cancellation of every ungodly trade made.

I request the cancellation of every ownership claim made upon me or my earnings ability.

I also request the cessation of any taxation to which I have been subject.

I forgive, bless, and release those who bound our generations by these oaths, vows, or covenants, in Jesus' name.

Await the verdict, then request access to the Court of Reclamation. In the Court of Reclamation, request to know what you can request specifically. You may need to visit this court successively over a period of time as this court does not release all you have lost to you at once. This court releases things stolen gradually.

———·———

Chapter 39
The Kingdom Dynamic of the Redemption Center

Some of you may remember the S&N Green Stamps you would receive for grocery purchases. You could collect these stamps in a book, take them to a Redemption Center, and exchange them for a toaster, mixer, or other items. Heaven has a Redemption Center as well, and because the good things on Earth are often patterned after what is already established in Heaven, I'd say Earth got the idea from Heaven.

It does not matter what was stolen; Heaven has provided for its return into your life.

Regardless of what has been lost, Heaven can restore it.

You may not receive the exact thing stolen, but the return will be comparable or better. What you lost in your twenties may not be as important to you in your forties.

Heaven can restore
what was lost to taxation or thievery
in some fashion.

Returning to our story of Stephanie and the Redemption Center, we were made aware that not only was restoration and redemption available for us, but it was also available for those involved as we were to witness in a short while.

First, let's find out what happened with the first ticket she was given. After the engagement with the Timing Devices, Stephanie was given three tickets for redemption at the Redemption Center. Having been overwhelmed at what Heaven had done moments before, Stephanie asked the Father to keep the three tickets until she was ready to redeem them.

Stephanie's Visit to the Redemption Center

Imagine if you will an enormous convention center, only the Redemption Center is much larger. It appeared to have multiple booths like you would see in an exhibition hall. Off to the side were walkways leading from the main floor containing more of the same.

A woman in white came to assist and led Stephanie to a hallway where the scenery changed as she stepped into it. She was surrounded by an aura with multiple shades of blue. Crystals were falling all around her but, at the same time, seemed suspended in midair. Our guide instructed Stephanie to look deeper.

As she did, she was engulfed even more in the aura, which was now a brilliant white. She was standing in light and was given the ability to see it in different ways. She saw a door, and stepping through it, she was back in the large convention hall.

She was instructed to look up. As she did, she saw the initial scene, but it seemed repeated at a 90-degree angle to where she originally stood. It was a new dimension of the same space. She instructed her spirit to step up into the new space. She saw rows of enormous vaults with open doors on all but the last one. She was prompted to go to the first one. She sensed that each vault represented significant time frames or events in her life when things were stolen from her.

As she stepped through the doorway of the first vault, she was a seven-year-old schoolgirl on her way to school. During that time in her life, a boy from school would often bully her by throwing rocks and soda cans at her, and sometimes she would get hit by these objects.

She was terrified about going to school. In the vision, she came to an intersection and decided which way to cross the street to avoid the boy. Jesus appeared with her and informed her that he had made it so the boy could never forget how he had treated her during that time. He showed that he was an extremely broken boy who suffered much abuse from his father. Jesus said,

---
Hurt people really do hurt people.

Then he asked her, "Would you allow me to use this instance to redeem a father wound in that boy?"

"Of course," she replied. She then began repenting on the boys' behalf. She forgave, blessed, and released him, then asked the Father to redeem the father wound. Jesus did something better; he made it as if it never were.

Stephanie then saw the boy pick up a rock, look at it, and put it down. He had decided to change his behavior. Jesus changed time for both Stephanie and the boy. He took away the enemies' ability to torment the boy and Stephanie. Then Jesus bent down and hugged the boy.

Stephanie walked back across the street and was suddenly older. The landscape changed as Jesus took a piece of His heart and placed it in Stephanie's heart. As He did so, she received a change of perspective.

Ron & Adina's Story

Stephanie began, "I would like to enter into the Court of Covenant on behalf of Ron Horner, please."

The attendant asked me, "You have made covenant that what you do for yourself, you do for Adina, right?"

"Yes," I replied.

The court attendants pulled both sets of records of our covenants with the Father (Ron's and Adina's). We were told there were six encroachments. We asked the scribe to show us the six. We took the paperwork and went to the Small Claims Court.

> We ask to enter the Small Claims Court in Jesus' name for Ron and Adina.
>
> Your Honor, we present to you six encroachments from the enemy.
>
> We could now see the enemy in the courtroom, but also other people behind the enemy. Six timing devices were brought forward and placed on a table before us.

On the first device, the light was off. We asked, "What is the encroachment that has been dismantled that we can claim."

We were told, "It was a territorial encroachment."

> We claim Ron and Adina's covenant around territories.

We moved to the second one. The light was on. It concerned something that occurred around the birth of their first child. It regarded disobedience of some sort.

We claim that obedience is better than sacrifice, and we make that claim in this Court of the Covenant.

The light went off.

We went to the next box. The third one was lit; it concerned relationships which are always centered around trust. This was generational—not just me or Adina. The attendant reminded us of the old saying that to *have* friends, you had to *be* a friend. The attendant pointed out that there were those in our generational lines that were not friendly—that did not treat others well.

Someone in the family line sought fame through friendships and relationships, which set up the family line for this Timing Device because of the fame they were seeking.

We asked, "Is it the word 'fame'? Is there anything around that at all?"

It's not the kind of fame we think of as being famous. They just sought the relationships through the relationships, not through the Father. They did not seek the Father.

We asked, "What is the repentance?" We were told to repent for the family members that sought fame instead of the Father. Repent for those in the generations who sought fame instead of the Father's friendship. As soon as we did so, the light went off.

We went to the fourth box. This concerned harboring animosities—unforgiveness. This, too, was generational. Ancestors were easily offended. It reminded us of Consequential Liens. Even though we have dismantled those Consequential Liens, the enemy still encroached upon the covenant.

I repent for those in my generations who harbored animosity as well as those in Adina's generations who harbored unforgiveness and animosity and were easily offended.

We repent for those deeds in Jesus' name. We ask your forgiveness, Father.

The light went off.

We looked at number five, where the light was off—this concerned profane worship, Freemasonry and two other deities or entities that have been worshiped. But the light was off. That indicated we had done generational work regarding these things. A Timing Device had been put there but was now turned off.

We claim the covenant relationship here with this one because Ron and Adina have done the generational work. In this Small Claims Court, we will claim that this covenant is intact with no further requirement upon them.

Now to the last one. The light was on. This one had to do with the judgment of others. It, too, was generational.

Father, we repent for those in my generations and Adina's who have been guilty of judging others and those that played God in their judgment, for those in my generations who played God over the lives of others.

We ask for forgiveness in Jesus' name.

That light went off.

We ask the angels to take these timing devices, dismantle them, and completely obliterate them in Jesus' name.

Redemption of the Timeline.

We were told by the attendant in the Small Claims Court, "Now, ask for the redemption of the timelines.

From this place, we claim the covenant relationships Heaven has designed for us.

We ask for the encroachments to be removed and for these Timing Devices to be dismantled.

We request the tickets to the Redemption Center.

We are asking for redeeming of the timelines here in time and out of time and in every dimension, in Jesus' name.

Six tickets to the Redemption Center were placed on the table, which we picked up.

We were interested to know who the people were that were located behind the enemy in the courtroom.

We were told, "Those in your generations that are not alive on the earth now."

We replied, "Thank you, your Honor."

"Thank you, Moses, for being our teacher. This is about how we are in covenant with the Father."

He said, "I enjoy teaching covenant. It is one of my favorite topics."

We replied, "Thank you, Moses."

The Process

- Request Wisdom's assistance
    - Identifying the problem.
    - Ask when was this placed on the family line?
- **Access the Court of Covenant**
    - Ask to see your scrolls containing any encroachments.
    - Offer repentance.
    - Receive paperwork from the Court of Covenant
- **Access the Small Claims Court**
    - Present the paperwork from the Court of Covenant
    - Request the Timing Devices be presented.
        - Repent for each encroachment.

- Request the shortening of the frequencies.
- Request redemption of the timeline

Chapter 40
The Kingdom Dynamic of Recognizing Your Gift

We had engaged with Heaven for Sandhills Ecclesia on a Thursday afternoon. Stephanie described what she saw. "Seth (a man in white we were introduced to in an earlier engagement and who is assigned to the Sandhills Ecclesia Intercessors) was tap dancing. He had dancing shoes on. He was really talented."

She asked, "Seth, what is happening with the tap shoes?"

He replied, "Would you think this is extraordinary?"

Stephanie responded, "I don't know how to tap dance, so, to me, it's extraordinary."

Seth asked, "Is it extraordinary?"

Stephanie replied, "I don't know. I'm still determining where we are going with this today, but this is very funny. Now, he is juggling."

Seth inquired, "Do you think this is extraordinary?"

Stephanie answered, "Again, I don't know how to do that, so, to me, it's extraordinary."

"Ah, I see where we're going with this."

Seth asked, "What about your gift? Do you think it's extraordinary?"

Stephanie replied, "I do, actually."

Seth continued his queries, "Well, what about those that don't have your gift? Do they think it's extraordinary? What about David's gift or Ron's? Is it extraordinary, or just who you are as a son?"

"If someone doesn't have a gift of sight, but they have the gift of prophecy, should they think your gift is extraordinary?"

Stephanie remarked, "I'm going to let you tell me this, Seth. I believe Ron's gift is extraordinary, but I don't have his gift."

Seth responded, "No, but you have your gift. Is it not equally as extraordinary?"

Stephanie commented, "It is from the Father, and yes, I would say so."

Seth asked, "Why do some discount the gifts the Father has given them, and only see the extraordinary in someone else?

---
*Sons must recognize
their gift...their gift!*

"Not a person in the ecclesia should discount their gift below another's.

"As you well know, a son is a son, no matter who the son is. Each is validated. Each is equal in the sight of the Lord. Seeking gifts is one thing—discounting your gift is another. Let no man esteem another's.

"I can tap dance, Stephanie, but you can sing. I can juggle, David, but you hear the heart of the Father. I'm here, and you're there, but I'm here doing extraordinary work and you're there doing extraordinary work. I'm a son just like you. Don't esteem my gift over another. Covet your gift. It is a gift from the Father. It is yours and yours alone. There is no one else that has the same gift that you have. Are there other gifts of sight or other gifts of prophecy? Yes, but are they the same? No. Just as the fingertips upon a man, each one is specifically different and unique."

Chapter 41
The Kingdom Dynamic of Being in the Father's Hands

This morning we met in the upper-level conference room in the LifeSpring business complex in Heaven. We had been taken to this room several times recently.

After greeting Wisdom, Lydia, and Malcolm, Malcolm announced, "The King is in the room!"

We thanked Jesus for coming, and as we did a deep reverence and peace permeated the room.

Jesus spoke to Stephanie and me, calling us "His Glory Makers of the Way."

Stephanie replied, "Thank you, Jesus. We say yes to you and all that Heaven has for your people, for Your Kingdom come and Your will to be done."

Jesus said, "There's a short tutorial for you."

Explaining what she was seeing, Stephanie said, "It's like when you start the first day of your job, and they give you a short introductory video to watch. It feels like that. We're going sit at this table, and I see the flicker of what you would see from an old movie before it starts.

"In the tutorial film, I see Jesus with the cross on his shoulder walking through the streets of Jerusalem before his death. I see his sweat and his blood. I see the thorns in his head and the weight of the cross. Oh, how heavy it was that day. I'm watching all the people around. He's showing me that some very young children were there, and on that day, innocence was stolen from them. They had never seen anything like that before. Now, I am being taken to the vision of the hole in the ground they would place the cross into. I see it. It's really deep. I can see into the ground."

Speaking to Stephanie, Jesus said, "It was someone's job to dig that hole. It was someone's job to build the cross that day."

Stephanie commented, "He's speaking of the enormity of that day though it seemed a normal day, to most, it was not. I have seen this hole that a person dug; it was their job."

Stephanie told Jesus, "Give us clarity and understanding of what you want us to know."

Jesus replied, "I want my sons to know that even on their worst day, their *worst* day, I have them in the palm of my hands.

> *I want my sons to know that even on their worst day, their worst day, that I have them in the palm of my hands.*

"I constructed through time the person I handpicked to dig that hole for the day of my crucifixion. Even on their worst day, I worked in them—for them. And if the sons let me, I will work through them.

Revelation is about understanding all the pieces, especially that which was meant for evil—the cross and killing me. All that was turned for good...the salvation of the world. Think for one minute about the person that dug the hole. That was his job.

How tough do you think it was for him when the reality came of who I am? Every day after that, it was tough for him to know he had dug the hole. The part he played set me up and lifted me up on the cross. He didn't know that he was part of the greatest plan. I walk in victory even because he dug that hole. My sons can walk with me in victory as they lie down their mindsets, struggles, and troubles and look at it through the lens of the one who had to dig the hole. My hand is upon all my sons as it was upon him."

Stephanie replied, "Thank you, Jesus, for this understanding. I have never once in my life thought about the person who did that."

He said, "You have no idea of even the smallest things done that day—things like digging a hole. Many other tasks like that were done by other people's hands."

Stephanie commented "Thank you, Jesus, for that." Jesus then leaned over, kissed Stephanie on the cheek, and left the room.

———·———

Chapter 42
The Kingdom Dynamic of Going Deeper

David and I requested a council meeting with Jonathan, Albert, Lydia, George, and others.

David began, "I see our book [the book of Sandhills Ecclesia]. It has been handed to us. Lydia has just come in. And she's saying, "David, the Father is excited about Sandhills Ecclesia, and the momentum that it has been given. In fact, the momentum will increase in the days ahead, and the resources will also increase as we need them." George agreed.

Remember to keep the flow of the Holy Spirit and the will of the Father. It is His desire to sup and commune with His sons.

The revelatory flow is the pulse of the Father's desire for Sandhills Ecclesia.

Speaking of the next Sunday gathering for Sandhills Ecclesia, George said, "There will be an increase of His presence as we wait on Him, as He manifests His glory. He will demonstrate his might and power greatly."

Lydia said, "As you know, Ezekiel captured the enemy's plan that had launched an all-out attack against you, but the frequencies have been cleared for manifestation like we have never known, but it was already ordained before the world began."

Lydia is smiling right now, and she's laughing with joy. She said, "All of Heaven is cheering you on. We who have been assigned to you—to Sandhills Ecclesia are rejoicing and celebrating with you, for the Father has given us a glimpse of His intended outcome."

Georgia stood and began speaking, "The currency angels have been assigned to release the wealth, the property, the land, and the deed. They are already stationed at the appointed place. They are assigned at the gates to bring [the provision]. David said, "I just saw two gates open. I can see what looks like Brinks armored trucks. I heard George say, 'Say it.'"

"Continue to enter the rest that the Father has spoken of and given you; it is a place of ease and peace knowing that your Father has everything in store and ordained. All things will be executed and delivered in the Father's timetable. I see the book [of Sandhills Ecclesia], and the pages are changing colors. Like strobe lights into multiple colors."

"George, what does this mean? David asked.

George replied, "What you see is the covenant of the Father with Sandhills Ecclesia. The colors are alive. They're vibrant. They're moving. They're vibrating."

David noted, "Now our book is back to the purple that it was initially. The pages are really alive."

"Yes," George replied, "The pages, the information, the revelation, the life, the flow of the Father, the intent of the Father, the will of the Father, the heart of the Father, the vision of the Father is all included and written in your book. It is His pleasure to give you the Kingdom because you have proven trustworthy, and you have stewarded what you have been given, and it pleases Him."

George then just tilted his hat on his head, turned, and walked away.

David asked those in attendance about the plans for Sunday. He said, "Any plans for Sunday?"

Lydia replied, "Go deeper into the revelation of the Glory. There's more that the Father wants to release and unfold to those who will be present. Teach the people that they are to dwell in the Glory of the Father. It is in your DNA.

Remember that you carry the DNA of the Father.

"When He breathed into Adam, He breathed into the DNA in Adam and this revelation, this awareness that...

The Father desires to bring back that which has been hidden regarding the Glory of the Father. He has chosen this to be released at this hour.

Lydia continued, "Take hold, steward, and possess the revelatory life that comes with the Glory of the Father. Impart and train. Pull. Draw out. For it is waiting to be released.

"You have used the term *Heaven on earth,* and now you shall experience it in greater measures and with understanding."

Malcolm's Instruction

Malcolm appeared, and David asked, "Malcolm, what do you have for us?"

Malcolm continued, "The Father says, "I have called Ron to the nations. And he must teach not just the local ecclesia, but I have called him and mantled him to teach the nations of your world."

David interjected, "I see Malcolm putting a gold quill- like a gold feather in your hand, Ron and I can see what looks like old scrolls, and you are writing."

Malcolm concluded by saying, "That's it for now." David replied, "Thanks, Malcolm."

David then explained, "Ezekiel is standing here not laughing, but with a smile. He has a look of agreement; he handed us a box." He said, "Take the lid off."

David asked, "What is in the box?" Ezekiel replied, "What do they look like?" "They look like books—like volumes. They look like volumes, not just regular books."

Ezekiel replied, "These are Books of Wisdom. Ron, you have been given the Books of the Wisdom of Solomon. The Father releases this today and the Spirit of Wisdom, one of the Seven Spirits of God, that God releases for you to navigate seamlessly. You are beginning a new season, and the Facilitator Training Program (FTP) class starts Monday. You will pour out wisdom into this new class. There will be things you would share with this class that you were not allowed to share before this time because you are in a different place.

Ezekiel continued, "Come on, my friend, you've got this. There's great acceleration for LifeSpring and Sandhills Ecclesia. My troops have increased, and we need more weapons and artillery, we need weapons for [dealing with] a water spirit. I want greater commissioning from Ron. My commanders and ranks have been added to. Many have upgraded in rank."

Ron began a request from the Father,

Father, I would request on behalf of Ezekiel, his commanders, and ranks: weaponry, artillery, cannons, harpoons, water cannons, water guns, arrows, crossbows, swords, spears, javelins, short swords, long swords, longbows, all the weaponry that he needs. We thank you, Father, for that. We thank you for weaponry, and for dealing with water spirits.

We commission you, your commanders, and your ranks to the full use of these weapons for the glory of God, for the ultimate and utter defeat of the enemy's kingdoms, his realms, and his dominions, in Jesus' name.

We commission you to guard the books, the volume of wisdom granted to me.

We commend you to the Father for your excellent service to the ministry.

We commission you regarding those newly added to the team in recent days so that you would encompass them with absolute knowledge of the presence of the angels of the Lord in their midst.

We request that you erect shields about them, their homes, businesses, finances, and all things that affect them, particularly their health in this season. Thank you for protecting everyone on the team and all those coming to the Florida conference.

We commission you to bring forth and release angels to minister protection and provision and release from fear concerning travel or concerning meeting together during February at Safe House Church in Fort Myers, Florida.

We commission you to work with Aprile and Chad and their angels and the angels of that house, the angels of Frank Sumrall and his wife Karen, in Jesus' mighty name.

We commission you to work with the angels of those assigned to come to this conference so that only those who are supposed to be there will come in Jesus' mighty name.

We commission you to arrange for safe travel, safe travel arrangements, safe housing arrangements, and to clear the houses and the properties where all will be staying (hotel rooms or wherever) and all necessary things, preparing the way for them and preparing Courts of Favor in their behalf as they get favor with their arrangements, with their travel, those sorts of things in Jesus' mighty name.

We also commission you to work with the currency angels to bring forth the provision needed during this season and worked together to bring the funds assigned to this house, to this ministry, to Sandhills Ecclesia, to LifeSpring

International Ministries and those involved in Jesus' name.

We commission you to help fulfill the assignments of that money destined into our hands to be distributed again into the Kingdom in Jesus' name, and on behalf of the Kingdom and for the glory of the Father in Jesus' name."

David noted what he saw happening to Ezekiel as the commissions were given. "As Ron did that, I could see Ezekiel as if he were growing up. Like he was lifting weights, like he was bulking up.

"I don't know if he is gold, for this is my first time really seeing him, but the more you talked about the Glory, the more golden his appearance became. It was if he, his commanders, and his ranks were being supercharged."

With that concluded, Ezekiel was gone. We were left to ponder the engagement of Heaven for this day.

———·———

Chapter 43
The Kingdom Dynamic of the Lens of Promise

Imagine a hot sunny day. You spray water on your driveway with a hose, and after a few moments, the sun evaporates all but a few pools. You walk to a pool of water and look into it, seeing your reflection. Sometimes reflections appear clearer than the original image.

Malcolm joined us in this engagement and encouraged us to look in the pool and tell him what we saw.

Stephanie said, "I want to look in and see Jesus."

Malcolm said, "Isn't that what the world is supposed to see? Are they not supposed to see Jesus when they see you? They are."

He paused and asked, "Why don't you see Jesus in you when you look in the mirror?"

Most of us are tough on ourselves and struggle with that.

Stephanie asked, "How do we see Jesus when we look at ourselves? When we are so hard on ourselves?"

He said, "That is the burning question."

Then he said, "Look deeper."

Stephanie looked again; this time, when she looked, she saw Jesus, but past Him, she saw the Father.

Malcolm commented, "This is abiding, isn't it? What did Jesus say when he said, 'When you see Me, you have seen the Father. If you know you are sons and abide in Jesus, and He abides in you, how do you not see Him when you see yourself in the reflection?"

Stephanie replied, "Because we have never been taught to look that way."

The Challenge

He said, "Put a challenge before the people to look at themselves in the mirror, eyeball-to-eyeball, and look to see Jesus.

"The point is to see yourself and see Jesus. See, He is there. As you have learned to live spirit-forward, learn to see Him in you as reflection."

We replied, "As we learn to do this and walk in this, people will see Jesus in us. We have often wondered how that can be—because we can be literal."

Malcolm interjected, "Sometimes it will be literal. Talk about a conundrum."

Stephanie remarked, "I liked this picture you gave us today, Malcolm. What will happen as we walk in this because it feels like a shift?"

He said, "Well, did it shift when you began living spirit-forward?"

"Yes," Stephanie replied.

"Did it shift when you began having the Glory stand up?" He asked.

"Yes." We replied again.

He said, "This is a shift. The title of this is *The Shift*.

"You have heard of people talking about transformation. Well, this will transformationally challenge. Those who do this will be challenged to call others to do it. That is the challenge. We do this, and then we challenge other people to do this. Thus, the transformation.

When you do this, and you look eyeball-to-eyeball in the mirror with Jesus, you cannot help but be transformed.

And when others look at you eyeball-to-eyeball, they will see and *want* the transformation."

And as we have borne the image of the man of dust, we shall also bear the image of the heavenly Man. (1 Corinthians 15:49)

But we all, with unveiled face, beholding as in a mirror the glory of the Lord, are being transformed into the same image from glory to glory, just as by the Spirit of the Lord. (2 Corinthians 3:18)

But be doers of the word, and not hearers only, deceiving yourselves. [23] For if anyone is a hearer of the word and not a doer, he is like a man observing his natural face in a mirror; [24] for he observes himself, goes away, and immediately forgets what kind of man he was. [25] But he who looks into the perfect law of liberty and continues in it, and is not a forgetful hearer but a doer of the work, this one will be blessed in what he does. (James 1:22-25)

———·———

Chapter 44
The Kingdom Dynamic of Being One with Creation

Stephanie said, "It's Adam. He's leaning against a tree and eating an apple."

Adam said, "This is the day that the Lord has made; you should rejoice and be glad in it."

Adam pushed himself off the tree with his shoulder and began walking. We could see through him as we had in another engagement. For the first time, we could see his curly hair—an auburn color. His skin, like other times we had seen it, was translucent in nature. When he swallowed the apple, we could see it going down his throat.

Stephanie asked, "What are you trying to say around, 'This is the day the Lord has made?'"

Adam replied, "The miracle of creation. If a day is as a thousand years and a thousand years is as a day with the Lord, imagine what day today is."

Stephanie remarked, "Okay. This should be fun! I will imagine with you, Adam. Will you take us down this imagination path? He is showing me something. It's as if we were looking outside the gates of the Garden of Eden into the expanse of the world. It is all very uncorrupted. There aren't buildings—it's just beauty."

Adam remarked, "The beauty of nature."

Stephanie commented, "I don't feel like we're going to walk outside of the entrance from Eden. We are *IN* Eden—that's what it seems like, but we're looking out at such glory!"

Adam added, "The glorious nature of creation."

Stephanie noted, "That's interesting that you said, 'The glorious nature of creation' because nature is a part of creation. Nature has multiple meanings here, doesn't it, Adam?"

Adam prodded, "Don't get sidetracked here."

Stephanie agreed, "I started going down the path of what nature means in my head."

Adam said, "It is true.

Nature is encapsulated within you.

You are the <u>very nature</u> of Christ.

"Not only does earth groan, creation groans for the sons of men, but the very nature of creation groans within you. It is the connection, the connectivity.

You will find that, molecularly, all of life is in you.

"All creation is in you as it is here in this place."

Stephanie added, "And when he said, 'Here,' the visual I got was—it's external, but it's also internal, and the understanding that I'm getting is that because all of creation and the nature of it is within us, we can connect externally with nature. Nature—that is external creation. That is how we're molecularly able to walk this out (and on top of it). Am I right?"

"When I said, 'Am I right?' he took a step, like he was going to step on stairs, but it was a cloud that he stepped on, and I'm watching him ascend, stepping on a cloud as if they are stairs. He stopped at the fourth cloud step, but he was still in the realm of what I would think of, near the ground, but he had ascended. Could you help me with this, Adam?" Then I heard Jesus' voice.

Jesus said, "These things that I did, you will do them and greater."

Stephanie noted, "I just got a picture of when Jesus ascended; when he was there on the mountaintop, I saw it as a picture of him taking steps into Heaven. He took a cloud staircase. It wasn't that he just flew, as we've always depicted him."

Stephanie continued, "Floating up; He ascended the stairs, he ascended molecularly; He was one with all creation. The visual that Adam gave me was the very visual that Jesus took that day.

"What do we do when we go up the stairs in the natural? We are ascending! He's encouraging me to climb. I'm going to do it. I can feel the sturdiness under my foot of what we would think of as a cloud that is not particularly sturdy, but I can feel my foot solidly on this. I'm taking the next step, and I'm standing on the same level as Adam."

Adam instructed, "Ascend!"

Stephanie remarked, "As soon as he said, 'ascend,' he disappeared, but the apple is on the stairs made of clouds with one bite out of it.

"I want to pick it up. I'm going to pick it up. I'm looking at this apple, and I don't see the apple. I see how it's made. I can see its molecular design. I can see the lines, the very inner workings. I can see through it partially. *Mechanics* is not the right word, but it feels like mechanics. It's the creation of it and what it's made of. And I see his bite mark, and I see the seeds. Adam is encouraging me to take a bite. I am to take the whole thing within me.

"I put the whole thing in me. The analogy I got the minute I did that was when we take of the apple; it becomes part of us. It becomes one with us as we chew on it, swallow, and digest it. It becomes a part of us, seeds and all. It's the analogy of being one with Jesus, one with creation, one with the earth, and how we will govern. It's a beautiful picture. Not just of, 'We are in Him, and He is in the Father,' but of all creation being in us. We are one with creation, which is how we will subdue the earth.

"Amazing. I can't see Adam anymore, but I can hear him."

Adam said, "This place (what feels like the Garden of Eden) is open to everyone. It's perfection, and everyone that is one with Christ has access to it and can walk through it at any time."

Stephanie added, "Interestingly, this garden feels very exclusive to me. I have a knowing that for anyone that walks through this garden, it will be exclusive to them, but yet, it's all the same garden. They're giving us little nibbles about how we can comprehend governing the earth visually.

———·———

Chapter 45
The Kingdom Dynamic of Good Fruit

Ezekiel came near, eating an apple. He had a basket full of apples with him and said, "It's the frequency of the sound of Heaven. There are truths on each apple. (Each apple had the word 'Truth' printed on it.)"

He said, "Why do you think people say, 'An apple a day keeps the doctor away'?"

Not knowing quite how to answer, we waited. Then, he showed the picture of how we know fruit is healthy as we look for bruises or evidence of insects. But he said, "How much more is truth to the body (meaning the body of Christ?)"

He paused, tossed an apple in the air, flew up, and grabbed and ate it. He had the basket of apples on his arm, and it felt like he was leaving to take these truths to everyone.

Father, we commend Ezekiel, his commanders, and ranks to you. And we thank you, Father, for truth, for the element of truth, for the frequency of truth, and for the baskets and baskets and baskets of it that you are bringing to our realms—to the people and their families and just for the joy of the engagement and how much fun you make it.

Stephanie remarked, "I see George, and his pants pockets are full of apples. One fell out as he was walking and rolled away. He went and picked it up and ate it.

"Now, Jesus came in, and they were laughing, and George and Jesus began throwing apples at one another, but they were catching them like you would catch a baseball."

She asked, "What is all of this about apples, Jesus, and George?" George said, "It's the fruit. You're bearing much fruit." Jesus said, "Listen to the sound."

Stephanie could hear people walking. She could hear many, many people's feet coming in our direction.

She remarked, "That's why George is here, isn't it?" Jesus' pockets were full. He walked up to Stephanie, took both hands, put them on my shoulders and said, "You're doing good, kid."

He smiled and waved at George as he walked away.

———·———

Chapter 46
The Kingdom Dynamic of Knowing the Gates of Hell Won't Prevail

Stephanie began, "I see Jonathan, and he's got a party hat on."

Jonathan replied, "Heaven enjoys celebrating its sons. As a matter of fact, Heaven constantly celebrates because there is no day or night here. It's continual."

Stephanie described what she saw, "Jonathan just showed me a very clear picture of the Father. He's just walking through what we would consider the streets of Heaven. And I see things like cafes and very casual eating places that people in the natural would go to. It's like that in Heaven. I see storefronts, and the Father is walking down the street, saying, "Hey, did you see my son David today!" And he is celebrating David (with everyone there). "Did you see my son Adina today? And they are all celebrating Adina. Did you see my son, Stephanie, today?" Heaven is always celebrating its sons.

Jonathan continued, "There's a misconception of how the Father views His sons, that He's sitting on this pious throne, looking through a book, making judgments and saying things like, 'Oh, David didn't quite make it today.' That is a huge lie and a misconception. The Father continually celebrates His sons. We need to remember that because of Jesus, his death on the cross, and the finality of that. The sons need to know the Father only sees them as completely righteous, completely clean, and able to come and stand boldly for before Him AS a son. Just as your sons would ask for the simplistic thing like, 'Hey, Dad, can I have the keys to the car?' Well, as a Father, you'll give that freely." Then he laughed and said, 'Well, to most sons, you'd give the keys to the car' (speaking of us in the natural)."

Stephanie said, "Yes, Jonathan. We do understand what you're saying."

Jonathan added, "If only the people could know the joy the Father has in each one of them. In His heart, upon His lips, are His sons. They are His sons—sons of the Most High."

Stephanie replied, "Amen. Thank you for that, Jonathan. We often get caught up in how we've made a mistake that day and how God must feel about us."

Jonathan said, "That is a lie from the pit of hell. It is a misdirection from satan because he knows...

> *Once the sons know who they are in their sonship, the gates of hell surely will not prevail.*

Stephanie responded, "That's interesting, Jonathan."

He said, "You often say, 'So that no man can boast.' Who could boast? Every son is on what you would deem the same level. Every son had the same access to the Father, the same level to the Father. The same joy the Father has for every son. The same celebration, unique to who you are, but sonship puts you all on an even plane. Knowing who you are as a son and knowing you are a son shakes the gates of hell. They won't prevail."

Stephanie remarked, "I'm seeing a common theme here over the last few days, Jonathan. Satan has tried to steal the idea of sonship from the sons, and we're taking it back through the Son.

Well, thank you, Jonathan. Thank you, Heaven, for using us, your sons, to bring this knowledge to your sons."

With that, Jonathan left with his party hat.

Chapter 47

The Kingdom Dynamic of a Governing Mantle

Immediately upon deciding to check in with Lydia, we were in the LifeSpring complex. We were standing at what appeared to be the front entrance. We noticed something above the door—the blood of Jesus had been applied to the door frame by the very hand of God.

Stephanie remarked, "I'm not sure why we're seeing that today. Lydia, what is this?"

Lydia laughed and said, "You are making it too complicated in your head. It's literally the hand of God on LifeSpring.

"Thank you, Father. Can you tell me the significance of why we saw that today?

Lydia replied, "His love. It's not just His love for us as individuals, but His love of this revelation, this work, and the entity that is LifeSpring. It's His work. There's great joy and love about the establishment of it in the Heavenly realms. It's a message of great pleasure in what is being done through the entity of LifeSpring. Great pleasure."

When Lydia said that the doors opened, and we walked in. We went to the Help Desk. Stephanie continued, "Why is Isaiah behind the Help Desk?" He had a book in front of him and was pointing to Isaiah 42:1:

> *Behold my servant, whom I uphold, my chosen, in whom my soul delights; I have put my Spirit upon him; he will bring forth justice to the nations. (ESV)*

Stephanie exclaimed, "Wow? Isaiah, thank you for showing us this."

We looked at the marble floor and could see that the verse was engraved into it. It reminded us of how the emblem of the CIA is embedded into the floor of the CIA headquarters building. This verse was embedded into the floor of the LifeSpring building.

Isaiah came from behind the desk and stood with us on the floor engraving. Suddenly we went into the words and whatever letter we were standing on; we were inside of it.

She asked, "Isaiah, can you tell me what I'm looking at, what we're in?"

Isaiah replied, "It's a picture of the scripture being embedded and ingrained in LifeSpring, the entity of LifeSpring. It's an embedded force of nature. It's an embedded force of creation—the very nature of God because you have said yes."

Stephanie explained, "He's now showing me scrolls. It's a picture of when he was here on earth, and he had the reality and understanding of the scrolls from Heaven. He learned to step on them. Step into them. That's how he received the knowing's that he had. The very nature of God would flow out of him from these places.

"He just turned and looked at me and he looks different now. His eyes are ablaze. He said, "You will now govern."

Stephanie replied, "We accept the 'now govern.' As he's walking away, there's this very long piece of material, it reminds me of what a wedding veil would look like. It's coming from off his shoulder. It's around his waist and up and slung over his shoulder. It's royal blue. It's a very long train behind him. We are still inside of this letter, and he is walking away. He's gone into the wall, but the train is left behind. Oh, my goodness. It's his mantle. I can hear him. He said, "Pick it up."

Describing the mantle further, Stephanie said, "It's so long. It's beautiful. It has its own movement. I just have the end of it, but I'm going to pull it towards us. It's going on forever as I'm pulling it towards me, instead of it just falling to the ground, it's going in me. And now I'm standing back on top of the letters and I'm back in the entrance of LifeSpring and the words are now under me.

I can walk on top of them and that's it. What is that? What just happened?"

I replied, "You've received an impartation from Isaiah. Stand to your feet for just a moment."

As she stood, she noted, "I feel the mantle across my shoulders."

Ron added, "Now let it become one with you and you with it."

Stephanie explained, "It's like a garment now. There's a long train behind me. Even when I hold my arms up, the fabric folds. The arms fold down towards the ground. Thank you, Father. Thank you. Your will be done. Father.

———·———

Chapter 48
The Kingdom Dynamic of the Master's Key

When Stephanie, David, Adina, and I stepped into Heaven on behalf of Sandhills Ecclesia, the first thing we heard was the phrase, "The Master's Key." We did not yet know who was speaking but knew that a master key would be one that would access all the locks of that particular style. It lets you open every door.

I wanted to know, "What is the Master's Key?"

Stephanie found herself in a scene that reminded her of Ireland. She could see rolling hills and green grass, and in front of her were two huge double doors that were closed. There was a stone wall along the pathway with stone laid upon stone. Some tether was midway through the door, strung from left to right across, and giant keys were hanging in the middle of the tether. She asked, "Is this the master key?"

She asked, "Are we supposed to take these keys? Because they look huge. They are bigger than I am," and finally, "Is the door in front of us locked?" These keys obstruct the view of the door. The keys are as large as eight feet tall from tip to tip.

Stephanie realized those were not the right questions.

I asked, "How do we obtain the master key?"

Heaven said, "It's right in front of you."

Stephanie remarked, "Okay, well, I cannot do this in my strength. I can't take the keys because they are so huge. Jesus, where I am weak, you are strong."

The keys immediately changed and fell into my hand. Now, the keys were the right size. They were the size of her hand. Okay. Jesus, because where I am weak, You are strong; I ask that you help me use the Master's Key to open this door.

Stephanie explained that the door had massive bricks laid across the top in a perfectly uniform manner, but it came down the sides. There was a covering over it, and there was moss everywhere. These were very ancient doors.

The door handles jut out about two feet. And there is an iron circle in which you can put your hand and finger, but the door is locked. She took the key, put it in the lock, and pushed it in. She could hear it going in and unlocking. She could hear many mechanisms inside this door as it was being unlocked. She asked David to help her pull the door open.

The Ancient Vault

Together they placed their hands on the handle, and as they pulled it, they felt a gust of wind when it opened. In front of them was a dark veil that kept them from seeing inside. Pushing the veil aside, they saw a vast hall with shelves on each side.

Stepping into the hall, David said, "There is an unlocking of the purpose of getting and receiving the keys. It unlocks something of great value but has not been available since the beginning."

Stephanie added, "In the past, we did not ask for His strength, and most people have not asked what the Father's heart is.

She inquired who was speaking to us and realized it was Wisdom.

We inquired, "Wisdom, will you guide us and teach us? Do we move forward from this place?"

Wisdom responded, "The master key and The Master's Key are the same. The master key is the original blueprint."

Stephanie realized, "It is more than just a key in our hand. It is a blueprint."

Suddenly the hallway turned into an enormous blueprint down both sides, on the floor, and the ceiling.

Adina remarked, "It reminds me of an ancient vault."

Stephanie added, "We are in a dimension because in this place, I feel like I am standing on glass and seeing the blueprint on the other side of that glass. Interestingly, the blueprint above reminds me of the sky at night. It is the blueprint of how and where He created and placed each star."

Wisdom interjected, "With pinpoint precision."

Adina commented, "I get that. This is an ancient vault with secrets rarely revealed to humanity because humanity would misuse the information if one had agendas. It is an honor for us to be shown this, for it to be opened. This is the blueprint of everything."

Stephanie said, "I have been instructed to walk over to the wall where there is one very long blueprint. I am to touch it." She did as she was instructed and her hand went right through the blueprint. She pulled her hand back out because she was not expecting that. She knew we could step through this wall showing the blueprint.

She remarked, "Wait, are you telling me, Wisdom, that when we are stepping onto the blueprint, we are stepping into what this is?"

Wisdom said, "Are you ready?"

David interjected, "The steps of the righteous are ordered."

Adina said, "The blueprint's already been created and designed. That is what I hear."

Stephanie asked Adina if she could also see it, and she could.

Adina said, "Yes, I see it. It was in the Ironman movie when he worked with his computer, his AI, and he enlarged the whole blueprint and he could stand in the middle of it and see it from all angles. He could see all of it. Everything."

Stephanie said, "Let us step in and see it from all around. When I put my hand into it, it was like another time or dimension, and my hand disappeared. Let us go because I am excited!"

Our Counsel

Stephanie took us all by the hand, and we stepped through the blueprint. We found ourselves in a Council Room.

All our council that we had ever met were in the room. We could see Einstein, Moses, David, Peter, John the Baptist, Elijah, Jesus, and Wisdom. We were standing together, and what we had seen as a blueprint was also a timeline. All of this had to do with time—with order.

It reminded us of the movie with Nicholas Cage, *National Treasure*, where they would go hunting for the treasures of the United States. They were always looking for the master key. It had nothing to do with keys; it was the blueprints he needed.

We paused before the council awaiting instruction.

David heard Jeremiah 29:11, which says, "I know the plans I have for you declares the Lord, plans to prosper you and not to harm you, plans to give you a hope and a future.

Stephanie noted, "Blueprints. Plans."

Adina remarked, "Codes. Keys are also called codes. A code to decipher something, A code to understand something. A secret code on a map like from *The Lord of the Rings*. There is always a code for a treasure map, and there will be a code to hide the information from those not worthy or those who would misuse the code. Get Wisdom. Wisdom unlocks the code, which is the key to the blueprint!"

The Chess Pieces

Stephanie commented, "I watched Jesus, who had a chess piece that was taller than a person would be. They were moving these chess pieces around. The color of all of this is that deep dark blue. We are standing in what we would know and see as a blueprint that is blue."

Adina reminded us that blueprints are made with blue ink.

Stephanie continued, "So when you were saying 'code,' the impression I got was that as they moved the chess pieces around, there was a strategic reason for each move. I am drawn to watch the King piece.

David asked, "You saw Jesus and someone else moving the chess pieces."

Stephanie answered, "Enoch was on the other side of Jesus. And there was also James. Jesus was on one side, and Enoch and James were on the other. And Jesus has the king.

Adina remarked, "Of course He does. He IS the king."

Stephanie added, "I want to know the significance. The first thing that popped into my head was through time, whatever the enemy came at us with, the King has always triumphed and always won."

David commented, "Yeah. The enemy is trying to move his pawns. But Jesus outplays him every time."

Stephanie asked, "Isn't there a key to chess?"

Adina remarked, "It can be a complex game. Very, very complicated. Very difficult.

Stephanie read, "To play perfectly, one must avoid making inaccuracies, mistakes, or blunders. These errors are usually due to some tactical oversight, such as time, overconfidence, or carelessness. Therefore, the key to chess is asking one question at a time. And the question is, 'Why did my opponent make that move?'

Stephanie admitted, "I know nothing about chess."

Adina interjected, "The queen is the most powerful of all. And checkmate occurs when the King cannot move, and you cannot keep your opponent from being able to capture the king. (And in this scenario, we are the queen.)

Stephanie, speaking to Wisdom, asked, "Will you give us insight on the chess moves that are being made? I know we are on a big timepiece. I know we are in the plans, and I know that all of you are here for a reason."

David added, "One main goal of chess is to gain an advantage over your opponent."

Stephanie continued, "I am glad you just said that because everybody I mentioned earlier, got in a single line, and they all took a step towards us. We were standing with Jesus. Jesus was standing there. He has the big King chess piece, and we are all on either side of him."

Someone in the room asked, "Are you willing to let Him move you on the chess board where he needs you?"

David heard the phrase, 'strategy in movement.'

Stephanie added, "The way we are positioned is two of us on His left and two of us on His right. And He's the checkmate mover. He is moving the pieces. And when he moves, he goes with each of us as he strategically puts us in play when we agree and say yes.

"We say yes to being moved. Enoch and James were trying to tell us earlier that they were pieces on the board, and we are pieces on the board."

David commented, "Listen to this chess strategy. It is a purposeful attempt to gain an advantage over your opponent. Unlike tactics, chess strategy involves long-term goals. It is usually related to having a safe pawn structure, space, and piece activity."

Stephanie continued, "Now I am seeing a picture of the original first picture of when we stepped in a couple of times for Sandhills, and we all saw the church at the top of the hill, and everybody is sitting at the bottom of the hill. All the people that are involved with Sandhills are here. It is a picture of them being here. And the question he is asking is, 'Are they willing?' We are in a specific time. We are standing in a dimension right now that is out of the time that we are in and on. What I am hearing is, David, when you read that, and you said 'tactics,' the enemy uses tactics!

"Jesus wants to know, "Are they willing to let him move them around on the chess board?" But as he moves each of us, I see it is not just us standing there; He's standing with us. He is that giant King. If they say yes, they need to know that it is Him moving them, and HE IS WITH THEM WITH EACH MOVE. Because the key we came in with was His strength and not our own. That is how we could even get here in the first place!"

Receive the Strategies

Stephanie continued, "All these people (in the council room) are still in the line, and each has a piece of something in their hand they will impart. They collectively walk up and place their piece at Jesus' feet.

They are giving pieces of themselves as a trade, and it is for us. Each has a strategy that they are imparting.

"I am supposed to start gathering these things up. They are strategies. I am picking up many of them and putting them in my heart. I came around to the front where Jesus was, and the big giant chess piece was in front of Him, and He had His right hand on it.

"We love that it is all you Lord, all of you. We are in awe of the king. We are in awe of the strategies. We are in awe of the privilege of being in this place.

"Wherever you move us on the board, thank you that you are also with us. (He's so much taller and grander than us in this particular picture.)

"I thank Heaven for Wisdom. Wisdom, thank you for being the key. I am feeling the instruction to step back out of the room and back into this ancient hallway. But we do not have to leave the room, nor do we have to go back out the door. They said door has been opened.

Re-engaging

Do we move down the hallway, or do we stay here? We get to come back into this place. To this exact place again. The idea is that we do not have to use the key to open the door again. The door's been opened, so that the next time we engage, we can step right back into this place. Thanks, Father. Thank You. You have entrusted us with this, and you trust us.

Adina remarked, "Well, the question for each of us, are we willing to let Him move us around on His chessboard? The question is not asking if you are willing to move to this area. That is not what it means. It means, are you willing to let Him move you and make changes in your life? It could be moving from one position to another or physically moving. Would you be willing to move from where you are in your relationship with Him to the next phase, to the next place in Him? Are you going to stay on the back row, never getting moved, never growing, never progressing, never being a part of what He is doing and wants to do through you?"

Stephanie said, "Daniel 2:22 and 28 records an important prophetic vision given to King Nebuchadnezzar. He said, 'There is a God in Heaven who reveals mysteries and reveals deep and hidden things.' Also, a verse in Deuteronomy 29:29 reads, 'The hidden things belong to the Lord our God. But the revealed things belong to us and our children forever. So that we may follow all the words of this law.'

"We are to seek out these things. He has permitted us.

"Really, what is given to us is the understanding to truly seek out the hidden things and what that can be like.

> We ask for the angels assigned to us to come near. Jonathan and Albert and all those that are under you, we ask you to go ahead of time and bring the ability for those that are coming Sunday to hear the message that they can seek out the hidden

things the Father wants and yearns and longs to reveal to His children. That they will understand that when we say 'yes' to allowing Him to move us where we need to be moved to, that He is with us, and it is in His strength only, and that we can trust it. And in the process, we are given strategies from so many of the cloud of witnesses. Instruct their hearts bring to them the knowledge, understanding, wisdom, and revelation, in Jesus' name.

"You know the master key in the natural unlocks all the doors. Whereas just a single key can only lock and unlock one door. You have a house, and you have a master key, and you have multiple doors that have different locks; the master key will unlock them all. I think that is pretty profound."

———·———

Chapter 49
The Kingdom Dynamic of Quantum—the Purest Form of Intimacy

Stephanie asked me, "When you hear that the Father has called someone to holiness, what does that mean to you?"

I replied, "I think of when Samuel's mother was praying for a son, promised to give him to the Lord and was told never to let a razor touch his head. His future son had been called to holiness."

Stephanie asked, "Is that different now that we are with the Holy Spirit and under the blood of Jesus?"

I answered, "He, the Father, is the one who makes us holy, but we make the determination to pursue holiness."

Immediately Stephanie said, "Well, I determine to pursue holiness as the Father has made me holy."

We then requested access to the realms of Heaven and asked, "What do you have, Father?"

Stephanie could see large cinder blocks, as if a partial wall was going up. It was longer at the bottom as it was in the process of being built.

She asked, "Can someone explain to me what this is?"

Malcolm appeared and asked, "How many walls do you think people have put up in the spirit against the Father?

"Reconciliation is about building bridges and not erecting walls. There is no sure foundation for erecting these kinds of walls against Heaven.

The sure foundation is found in the completeness of one's identity to who they are in Christ.

"Let's talk about spiritual domains."

Malcolm was leaning against the wall, and I asked him, "How can we take the wall down?

"As the people have been moving through generational cleansing, these walls come down."

He took off the first top cinder block and laid it down.

He continued, "Continue through the constructs of time. Generations have been building walls against the Father, not piece by piece. So that is the first step.

Stephanie commented, "I see three cinder blocks. It is as if He is going to pull them all off at the same time. How is that done?"

Malcolm replied, "Through purging old mindsets and religious thinking they will be dismantled."

Stephanie could now see two cinder blocks.

Malcolm said to her, "You are about to remove them."

She asked, "How can we remove that one?"

Malcolm explained, "These are here because of the lack of praise and worship, adoration, gratitude, and bestowing upon the Father and the Son, the recognition for what has been done."

He pulled that block down and is now standing on top of five.

The first layer of this was the lack of desire.

Suddenly, there is a portal open. He asked, "Are you ready to go further?"

"Yes. Malcolm, thank you for the initial first steps," we replied, we are going to walk through this portal with you, and we can see it is a long tunnel, but we see it moving around us as if it were alive. We opened our eyes and could see no obstructions in front of us. We were in the realm of intimacy.

> *To understand physics,*
> *you must first understand intimacy.*

He said, "If Father created time and space, would he not have done so in intimacy with time and space?

"When something is lovingly created, there is an intimacy to it. That is why people can walk in the intimacy of the Father because they are in time and space. He created it. The practicality of all of this is to understand it is all relevant. The cry of intimacy far outweighs the building blocks set against time and space.

> *Quantum is the*
> *purest form of intimacy.*

> *Without quantum undoing,*
> *the done could never be done.*

"There would be no intimacy with his people. He loves them so much. He can do these things under his constructs without physics.

> *There could be no intimacy*
> *without physics.*

> *Without intimacy,
> there could be no physics.*

"It's all relative." He said, "Chew on that one."

Stephanie replied, "Well, I will have to because I have no idea what you are talking about!"

Malcolm asked, "What do you see here?"

She replied, "I see light. It's literally all light."

He turned to Stephanie and said, "What do you see here?"

She answered, saying, "I see a distinct color light, and I see jewels, and I see stones."

He turned her another way, and she could not see anything, but I knew it was the beginning of something newly formed and created.

Malcolm said, "Father has intimacy with his new creation. He is always forming. He is always creating; you can share the intimacy with Him co-created one. Step inwards, outwards, and upwards. Defy."

We asked, "How do we defy physics If it is relative, and it is intimate?"

He replied,

> *When you are in Heaven,
> you can defy physics.*

Stephanie replied, "I'm game. Help me to defy physics."

He explained, "To do so, you cannot only think about one plane—the earth plane. Be in Heaven and on earth simultaneously, and you can defy physics. That is where intimacy is because you can be on earth and in Heaven simultaneously. You have heard this. You know this. You have even had little exercises in it."

We asked, "So how do we do this day in and day out?"

He replied,

---

*Know that in both realms,
there is much intimacy
with the Father.
Draw from its light.
Everything is light.*

Stephanie responded, "Well, Father, I seek to stay in your light in this earthly realm and the heavenly one at the same time and to move in it and to walk in it."

Next, we were shown a mirror in a mirror. Looking into the mirror, Stephanie said, "I see a line down the whole middle of me, literally. One side of me is in Heaven, and the other is on earth. One foot is on earth. One foot is in Heaven."

Malcolm asked, "How could you get off the golden path with one foot in Heaven?"

Stay here in these places. This is your rulership. Defy physics."

With that, he was gone.

———·———

Chapter 50
The Kingdom Dynamic of Ordered Steps

As we began this engagement with Heaven, Jesus could be seen stepping on large land masses. We realized he was stepping on states. He wanted to teach us about ordered steps which he described as an agreement.

Even though we may have been commissioning our angels to order our steps, we must also be in agreement with the work they do in the process.

If we agree with the ordered steps of the Lord, we can conquer entire states.

In the Old Testament, when Kings would conquer an area, they would set about to govern it. The conquered area came under the governance of the king who conquered it.

> *If you formulate the conquering,
> it becomes a governing.*

To formulate means to methodically create or devise a strategy or a proposal to express an idea in a concise or systematic way. Those are two of the definitions.

If we express the idea of conquering in a systematic way through ordered steps, we can govern.

> *How can two walk together except they agree. (Amos 3:3)*

We should never formulate any point or step anywhere on any territory without consulting Jesus first. It must be done via an active agreement because it is agreement with Jesus.

> *In all our ways, acknowledge him and he will direct our paths. (Proverbs 3:6)*

If we acknowledge Jesus concisely and systematically, He will direct our paths. When He directs our paths, then we govern. We conquer, and then we govern.

Jesus has engineered it to be this way.

When something has been engineered, it has been skillfully and deliberately arranged rather than arising naturally or spontaneously. Jesus *skillfully and deliberately arranges the agreement*. We must have ordered steps that express concisely and systematically the way we conquer, then govern.

The steps of the righteous are ordered by the Lord. (Psalm 37:23)

Every place that the sole of your foot will tread upon I have given you, as I said to Moses. (Joshua 1:3)

Jesus wants to walk on every state in agreement with us.

As we follow His ordered steps, our steps are ordered as well. It can't be anything we have conquered. That's the ease in it. We have been busy trying to conquer things ourselves, but the ease is that He has ordered the steps, but we must be in agreement with it.

This is where excellence steps in. This is where the Bond of Excellence is important—stepping into the Spirit of Excellence because this is about steps! Step into the Spirit of Excellence and walk in lock step with Jesus to conquer our state or province.

We are not the initiator—He is. We just have to agree with the direction He is taking or be sensitive to the direction—discerning the direction.

This is a whole lot easier than people who want to do it through warfare—the swinging of the swords and all those things because they decide to take a territory or take the city, and they aren't the ones to do it, or they aren't prepared to do it, or they aren't strong enough to do it. Maybe there are not enough of them to maintain it.

Every commandment which I command you today you must be careful to observe, that you may live and multiply, and go in and possess the land of which the LORD swore to your fathers. (Deuteronomy 8:1)

Many think they can do warfare against principalities the old paradigm way, and you end with so much backlash that now there are only a few people out there standing in their place. Some are even out of church, and it knocks some of them out of doing intercession work because of trying to do things a much harder way. But seeing this, Jesus is not straining to step on those states, and his foot covers every state completely.

Now I saw Heaven opened, and behold, a white horse. And He who sat on him was called Faithful and True, and in righteousness He judges and makes war. (Revelation 19:11)

We must do the necessary court work to ensure victory on the battlefield. Many have gone to battle, never having inquired of the Lord for the necessary verdict from the Courts of Heaven. Jesus understands the process—court work, then battlefield work. We have found that warfare is no longer required if we do the proper court work.

How beautiful are the feet of them that bring good news. (Isaiah 52:7)

The Father has already strategized and ordered our steps FOR us, so if we agree with Him, rather than saying, "I don't want to move over there, I don't want to do this, I don't want to do that,"—if we are walking in rebellion, or whatever. He is saying, "Be yielded to me, let me bring you into doing what steps I have ordered because Heaven is waiting on us. Heaven is waiting!"

Look at the people that are now being impacted. He is ordering our steps and all we must do is agree with it and walk in it and then see what He does with the beautiful theme of the good news of the gospel of Jesus Christ and the life-changing messages and revelation that he's given that we don't have to do things a complex way.

---

*If He has ordered our steps
and we come into agreement with it,
He is actually taking the steps, not us!*

We have begun saying, "Glory, stand up, Glory, stand up, Glory stand up!" Then we begin to move from glory standing up to stepping into the glory. Stepping into the glory. From there, we begin to see a blueprint, and put our hand in the blueprint (the orders—the directives and the plans for our life). When we step into the blueprint, we become engulfed in the blueprint. We become the blueprint!

In becoming one with the blueprint of the Father for our lives, we find our steps ordered, and we then step into the mode of conqueror, and then governing son. It's an exciting journey! Let's not miss a single step.

———·———

Appendix A

The Kingdom Dynamic of Accessing the Realms of Heaven

A tremendous privilege we share in this time in history is the ability to easily access the realms of Heaven. Many of us were taught that Heaven is only for after you die. Heaven is more than a final destination on a journey, but can also can be a vital aspect of that journey.

What I am about to share is vital in progressing in the various Courts of Heaven. We can access the Mercy Court in the heavenly realm while fully planted here on the earth, but to maximize our endeavors in the Courts of Heaven, we need to learn how to operate FROM Heaven.

In teaching on accessing the realms of Heaven, I often point out some simple facts. If you were to tell me you were a citizen of a particular town, but you could tell me little of it from your personal experience, I would doubt the authenticity of your citizenship. I am a citizen of a small town in central North Carolina. I am familiar with the location of the city hall, police station, hospital, local county courthouse, Sheriff's Department, and much more. I know where many sporting events will be held. I know where the parks are. I know many of the stores and restaurants. I am familiar with this small town. Yet, if I ask the average believer what they can describe of Heaven from personal experience, the answer will likely be nothing. They have no personal experience of Heaven that they can relate to me. It does not have to be like that.

In Matthew 3, Jesus informed us that the Kingdom of Heaven was at hand. You could say, "The Kingdom of Heaven is as close as your hand." Hold your hand up in front of your nose as close as you could. Do not touch your nose. Heaven is closer to you than that. It is not far, far away up in the sky. It is not "over yonder," as some old hymns describe. It is a very present reality separated from us by a very thin membrane—and we can access it by faith. It is very simple.

When Jesus was baptized in the River Jordan, as He came up out of the water, IMMEDIATELY the heavens were opened. He both saw (a dove) and heard (a voice coming from Heaven). This one act of Jesus restored our ability to access Heaven. We can experience open heavens over our life. We don't have to wait. We can live conscious of the realm of Heaven and live out of that reality!

> *Everything we do as believers
> we must do by faith.*

Accessing the realms of Heaven is done the same way. Prophetic acts can create realities for us. It is the same with this. You can visualize stepping from one room into another easily. It is like stepping from one place to another. To learn to access the realms of Heaven, you will follow the same pattern.

Stand up from where you are now and prepare to work with me. You can experience the realms of Heaven right now! You don't have to wait until you are dressed up in a long box at the local funeral home or decorating an urn. You can experience Heaven while you are alive! Remember, we enter the Kingdom as a child.

Quiet yourself down. Turn off distracting background noises if possible. Prepare to relax and focus. Now, say this with me:

> *Father, I would like to access the realms of Heaven today, so right now, by faith, I take a step into the realms of Heaven. [As you say that, take a step forward.] Imagine you are going from one place to another in a single step. Once you have done so, pay attention to what you see and hear. You may see very bright lights; you may see a river, a pastoral scene, a garden—any number of things. Right now, you are experiencing a taste of Heaven. You will notice the peace that pervades the atmosphere of Heaven. You might notice the*

air seems electric with life. The testimonies I've heard are always amazing and beautiful to hear.

Now spend a few minutes in this place. Remember, Jesus said that to enter the Kingdom you must come as a little child. I often coach people to imagine yourself as an 8-year-old with what you are seeing. What would an 8-year-old do? He or she would be inquisitive and ask, "What is this? What does that do? Where does that go? Can I go here?" If a child saw a river or a lake, what would that child want to do? Most would want to jump in the water.

The variety is infinite. The colors—amazing! The sounds are so beautiful. You can learn to do this on a regular basis. When you access the realms of Heaven, you are home. You were made to experience the beauty of Heaven.

The reason learning to access the realms of Heaven is crucial to engaging the Courts of Heaven is that much of what we do is done FROM Heaven. We need to learn to engage Heaven and work from it.

Many people tell me they can't "see" visually in the spirit. Often, they are discounting the ability they do have. They may be discounting their "knower." Every believer has a "knower" at work within them. This "knower" who is Holy Spirit at work within you helps you to perceive things. Whether something is good or evil, He works to guide you more than you may have realized. Most navies that have submarines have a device known as sonar. Sonar gives a submarine "eyes" to see what is in their vicinity. They can detect what the object is by the ping emitted by the sonar. They can determine the distance to the object and if it is another submarine. They can even identify what class of submarine it might be. Sonar is invaluable in this setting, but a video camera would be rather useless underwater.

The military has a similar device for above ground situations known as radar. It functions in much the same manner. If a pilot were flying through thick cloud cover, the pilot would need to know what is in his path. Radar becomes his eyes.

Some people function visually. They often see what amounts to pictures or video images when they "see" in the spirit. They may see more detail. Yet one operating by his or her "knower" (their spiritual radar or sonar) can be just as effective as a seer. If you operate more like sonar or radar, don't discount what you "see" in that manner. It is how I function, and I have been doing this type of work for many years.

I can often detect where an angel is in the room (or if it is one of the men or women in white linen and not an angel). I can often detect how many are present and whether they have something they are to give to someone. I can detect any number of things and even though it is not "visual," it is still "seeing." It will set your mind at ease when you understand that operating by your knower is just as valid as any other type of vision. It will help you to realize you have been seeing much more than you know and you may know much more than some who only see.

Be willing to take a step right now into the realms of Heaven. You will be amazed at what you experience. You should sense a change in the atmosphere around you as well as sense the peace of God in an amazing manner. Enjoy the journey.

References

Strong, J. (n.d.). *Strong's Concordance.*

Description

Heaven keeps pouring out insights and revelation for the maturing of the sons of God. No longer will we settle for the status quo. Those clothes don't fit any longer. We have been made Kings who are priests, and we have a responsibility to establish on earth that which is in Heaven.

Old methods won't suffice, nor will old paradigms. We must engage Heaven for the new, the fresh, the life-giving riches and wisdom of Heaven. Learn how to engage and hear from Heaven's spokespersons. Learn to govern as a son!

About the Author

Dr. Ron Horner is an apostolic teacher specializing in the Courts of Heaven. He has written over thirty books on the Courts of Heaven, engaging Heaven, working with angels, or living from revelation.

He currently trains people in engaging the Courts of Heaven in a weekly online teaching session. You can register to participate and discover more about the Courts of Heaven prayer paradigm on his various websites, classes, products, and services found here:

www.ronhorner.com

Other Books by Dr. Ron M. Horner

Building Your Business from Heaven Down

Building Your Business from Heaven Down 2.0

Building Your Business with the Blueprint of Heaven

Commissioning Angels – Volume 1

Cooperating with The Glory

Courts of Heaven Process Charts

Dealing with Trusts & Consequential Liens

Engaging Angels in the Realms of Heaven

Engaging Heaven for Revelation – Volume 1

Engaging Heaven for Revelation – Volume 2

Engaging Heaven for Trade

Engaging the Courts for Ownership & Order

Engaging the Courts for Your City (*Paperback, Leader's Guide & Workbook*)

Engaging the Courts of Healing & the Healing Garden

Engaging the Courts of Heaven

Engaging the Help Desk of the Courts of Heaven

Engaging the Mercy Court of Heaven

Four Keys to Dismantling Accusations

Freedom from Mithraism

Kingdom Dynamics – Volume 1

Let's Get it Right!

Lingering Human Spirits

Lingering Human Spirits – Volume 2

Living Spirit Forward

Overcoming the False Verdicts of Freemasonry

Overcoming Verdicts from the Courts of Hell

Releasing Bonds from the Courts of Heaven

Unlocking Spiritual Seeing

SPANISH

Cómo Proceder en la Corte Celestial de Misericordia

Las Cuatro Llaves para Anular las Acusaciones

Liberando Bonos en las Cortes Celestiales

Liberando Su Visión Espiritual

Sea Libre del Mitraísmo

Tablas de Proceso de la Cortes del Cielo

Viviendo desde el Espíritu

www.ingramcontent.com/pod-product-compliance
Lightning Source LLC
Chambersburg PA
CBHW022000160426
43197CB00007B/198